Out the Window

Out the Window

Liza Balkan

Luminato production created in collaboration with:
Sarah Garton Stanley, Syrus Marcus Ware, Rosina Kazi,
Nicholas Murray and the company

SCIROCCO DRAMA

Out the Window
first published 2022 by Scirocco Drama
An imprint of J. Gordon Shillingford Publishing Inc.
© 2022 Liza Balkan

Scirocco Drama Editor: Glenda MacFarlane
Cover design by Doowah Design
Cover photography: Kyle Purcell

Photo of Liza Balkan by David Spowart
Photo of Sara Garton Stanley by Tracey Erin Smith

Printed and bound in Canada on 100% post-consumer recycled paper.
We acknowledge the financial support of the Manitoba Arts Council and
The Canada Council for the Arts for our publishing program.

Production inquiries to:
Ian Arnold
Catalyst TCM Inc.
#312-100 Broadview Avenue
Toronto, Ontario, Canada
M4M 3H3
ian@catalysttcm.com

Library and Archives Canada Cataloguing in Publication

Title: Out the window / Liza Balkan.
Names: Balkan, Liza, author.
Description: A play.
Identifiers: Canadiana (print) 20220196761 | Canadiana (ebook) 20220196834 |
ISBN 9781927922927 (softcover) | ISBN 9781990737145 (HTML)

Classification: LCC PS8603.A45 O98 2022 | DDC C812/.6—dc23

J. Gordon Shillingford Publishing
P.O. Box 86, RPO Corydon Avenue, Winnipeg, MB Canada R3M 3S3

To Franco Boni and The Theatre Centre, Toronto.
To Aislinn Rose and The Theatre Centre, Toronto.
Thank you for your belief, encouragement,
generosity, and patience.

Thank you for forever shifting my definitions of
"theatre," "process," "home," and "community."

Thank you for giving me space and time to investigate,
learn, unlearn, relearn, fail, regroup, mess up, and
perhaps begin to grow as an artist and a citizen.

And to my sister, Donna Balkan. Gone way too soon.

Out the Window
A Project. A Process. A Play. A Production.

In August 2000, Liza Balkan witnessed the beating death of a man named Otto Vass during an altercation with the police in the west end of Toronto. Called to the witness stand on a number of occasions over several years, Balkan kept careful track of the aftermath, then turned verbatim court transcripts, audio, video, and text derived from multiple interviews with lawyers from both sides of the bench, officers, family members of the deceased, activists, and artists, into *Out the Window*. This is a documentary theatre project that interrogates the subjects of policing and police violence, use of force, mental illness, racism, justice, memory, witnessing, and theatre. It was created to be a malleable, inclusive theatrical investigation, one that has evolved over many years, responding to the times and to the layers of the harsh realities around police violence and calls for change. Its storytelling vibrates in the past and in the present.

Out the Window is both a highly theatrical play and a public forum; a conversation—one that aims to continue forward. This book chronicles this project's process through its various iterations and includes the script from The Theatre Centre/ Luminato Festival co-production in Toronto in 2018, directed by Sarah Garton Stanley.

Liza Balkan

Liza Balkan is an Ontario-based, multi-disciplinary theatre artist whose practices and artistic inquiries continue to evolve as she heads into her fortieth year in the profession. She works as an actor, director, librettist, writer, and educator. She has written text for music works produced by Tapestry Opera, Bicycle Opera Project, Opera McGill, Brooklyn Art song Society (NYC), Scrag Mountain Music (Vermont), and Five Borough Songbook 2 (NYC). In collaboration with composer Paul Shilton, Liza recently created, wrote, and directed the verbatim song cycle *So, how's it been?* which had a sold-out run at the outdoor Here for Now festival in Stratford, Ontario during the summer of 2021. She also wrote the text for composer Brian Current's new opera *Gould's Wall*, in production in 2022 at Koerner Hall / RCM.

During a multi-year Residency at The Theatre Centre, she developed her documentary / verbatim project *Out the Window*. Liza directed its original production at The Theatre Centre, and it was produced at Toronto's International Luminato Festival in 2018, directed by Sarah Garton Stanley. Early written works include her solo shows *BRANGST*, and *Leftovers*, performed at assorted festivals and fringes across Ontario. Liza's recent directing credits include *Much Ado about Nothing* for Canadian Stage's Shakespeare in High Park, *Every Brilliant Thing* (starring Rebecca Northan) at Grand Theatre in London, and the premiere stage production of Stephanie Martin's opera *Llandovery Castle* at Opera Laurier. Liza has been an actor in multiple productions across Canada and in the US. She received a Dora Award for her performance in Theresa Tova's *Still the Night* (Theatre Passe Muraille / Tapestry).

Playwright's Notes

I didn't know Otto Vass. I walked by his antique/junk shop down the street every day. I had never gone in. Never met the man. Didn't know the man. The first time I met him was from my window on August 9th during his final minutes on this planet.

During a rehearsal for the 2018 production of the show at the Luminato Festival in Toronto, I was asked if I wished I hadn't been home that hot, summer night in 2000. It's a good question. Interestingly, with an event that had me dog-paddling in a sea of questions and transcripts for so many years, I must admit that this particular query was never really on tap. My first answer was—and still is—that of course I wished, more than anything, that it hadn't happened at all; that Mr. Vass hadn't encountered his death that night in a parking lot in front of the 7-Eleven. My second answer was that in fact, I felt fortunate to have been there; to have been drawn to the window by the yelling I was hearing outside, and to become witness to Mr. Vass's death at the hands of four police officers. It gave me an opportunity to step up and begin an essential voyage of learning, creativity, and gaining deeper understanding about many things. Over many years.

Had I been more aware that night of how my own white privilege played into my lack of a more layered comprehension of policing and the justice system, I wonder how this project, created over so many years, might have taken a few different routes along the way. As it is, *Out the Window*'s journey involved multiple twists and turns, informed by time, events, grit, collaborations, support, research, residency, belief, and community.

Out the Window is a project, a play, a conversation, a meal, an investigation, a gallery, a provocation, a dance party, a call to action, and a reach for community. It began in 2007 as an art project/performance installation at Lab Cab: a multi-disciplinary arts festival set in and around Toronto's historic Factory Theatre.

It travelled through many iterations on its road to the 2018 production at the Luminato Festival, Toronto's International Festival of Arts and Ideas.

When Glenda MacFarlane got in touch with me to say that Scirocco was interested in publishing the play, I felt excited, honoured, grateful, intrigued and… concerned. This is a project that has proven to be the most malleable of creative endeavours— each time shared differently from the last. Its malleability is an intrinsic aspect of the piece. Each showing in the course of its development has been unique. My hope for the project has always been that it would respond to the times and also visions of those who might choose to take it on. Sharing the script from the 2018 production was a thrilling prospect. It was guided, developed and directed by incomparable director and artist Sarah Garton Stanley. It embraced new creation and perspective that reflected the urgency of the time in which it was produced for—and with—an audience; an urgency that continues.

And yet. The question that arose was: How to capture a project that is both a play and a communal conversation that lives simultaneously in both theatrical and real and present time? This has always been the intended malleable nature and shifting form of *Out the Window*.

It was through a conversation with Franco Boni, former artistic director of The Theatre Centre in Toronto, that an idea emerged around the possibility of sharing aspects of its journey. Given its multiple and varied iterations, and how deeply each outing has been informed by its predecessor, I wondered if the publication of its 2018 production script might also include information and perspective about its continued developmental process and performances over the years. It is rare to be given the opportunity to share publicly a reflection of a project's process. Theatre creation is all too often focused on "product." *Out the Window* was a constant practice in the art of "process." This is owed entirely to The Theatre Centre, who first gave the project Residency: time and space in which to begin to investigate its creation with others. I was overjoyed when Glenda and Scirocco said yes to this idea. Also: nervous. There's a lot of material. However, anyone who has created projects in the verbatim genre knows well the valuable, prime real estate of the cutting-room floor.

Alongside the script, this book includes some information about the project's history, bits of material from a couple of its earlier showings. and thoughts and perspectives from a number of people who have been involved in various aspects of the development of the project over several years. You will find a few words shared by Franco, The Theatre Centre Artistic Director Aislinn Rose, Sarah Garton Stanley, artist and activist, Syrus Marcus Ware, Luminato Artistic Director Naomi Campbell, designer Trevor Schwellnus, and actor Brett Donahue. I am chuffed beyond measure to have their perspectives included within these pages.

The view from my window. Photo by Trevor Schwellnus.

Acknowledgements

The list of thank-yous is a long one. You will find it amongst these pages. In the meantime, I will begin with a very huge thanks to Glenda MacFarlane and Karen Haughian of Scirocco Drama/J. Gordon Shillingford Publishing Inc. I am forever grateful to have the opportunity to share this material and to pass it forward. Thank you to Sarah Garton Stanley, Syrus Marcus Ware, Trevor Schwellnus, Naomi Campbell, Brett Donahue, Aislinn, and Franco, for so generously taking me up on the invitation to share some thoughts about this project.

The Text

The text in this project and play is comprised primarily of edited court transcripts and interviews. There is also a smattering of created dialogue thrown in for good measure.

The court transcripts themselves were obtained either through purchase, or, as is the case with my own testimony as a witness, provided to me either through my own request or else forwarded to me by the court system in order to prepare for the inquest in 2006.

I received permission from those interviewed to use their interview material.

Like most projects that utilize verbatim material, the process took a goodly number of years of research, sorting, culling and editing of hundreds upon hundreds of transcribed court proceedings and interviews. Many of these pages are still in boxes in a basement. Letting go of them all has proven to be tough. I dunno. Perhaps this publication will finally allow me to lay them to recycled rest. Maybe.

Director's Notes
Sarah Garton Stanley

It's 2022 now. The world has changed a lot since the summer of 2018. It makes it even harder to look back at this story, one that details the arc of brutality in Toronto's early 2000s, and not get misty-eyed for how much less brutal things seemed then.

The murder of Otto Vass at the hands of the police and as witnessed by Liza Balkan was brutal. The court proceedings that followed and the outcome for the officers are in some ways as predictable as any of the many courtroom dramas on Netflix. The loss of life and, I believe, a level of innocence in Liza Balkan's life will never be recaptured. The systems that we, as a society, have chosen to support, are vested with the power to take a life, to legally support that taking, and finally, to diminish the ideals of its citizenry. It is a system that we all support through our taxes. What to do?

When Franco Boni approached me about the possibility of directing a next iteration of Liza's *Out the Window*, I was filled with hesitation.

Truth be told, I wasn't into it. The story of a senseless murder and a witness to that crime was important, compelling and heart wrenching…but after a spate of police brutality in the intervening years since Otto Vass's death, I had to ask: What's the point? We know the cops and the system that supports them are brutalizing and dehumanizing, we know that the legal system works from precedent, not justice, and we know that Otto Vass is dead. What can we offer by bringing this story back to life once more?

I feel a responsibility as a storyteller to seek to find true places of transformation both for the subjects and for the audience. I was struggling to find the movement in this terrible story of intransigence. But it got me thinking…what might happen if we play the fuller text in a shortened one-act version? With this truncation we can almost get operatic in the pain and suffering and draw on fascist lines to relay the contours of what happened. Make it glisten in its awfulness. And then take a break and figure out how as a community, actors and choir, along with the audience, can build together a communal experience that requires the involvement of everyone. I wanted to create a big space of "hug" for those willing to sit in the troubling questions.

And… I also had a secret wish… from the moment I decided to do the show…to somehow create the circumstances that would find many of the audience on the stage taking a bow along with the performers at the end. It happened.

I cried every night at the sight of this alchemical occurrence. It was, I believe, transformative. And furthermore, I believed that the audience left the experience renewed, reinvigorated and ready to fight, or at the very least, to agree to be a witness to the horrors and the beauty of life. The theatre can be a place to recharge and its rituals can help unlock our inner resistance to change—or perhaps, more persistently, it can help us imagine possible worlds through recounting worlds of limited possibility. We, together, mourned Otto Vass. We, together, shared in the pain Liza Balkan sustained as a witness. Most importantly, we sat together amid the current shame and pain of 2018, when the irrefutability of Black Lives Matter and Indigenous sovereignty were being questioned and diminished by the same brutalizing systems that lent ammunition to the murder of Otto Vass. We must stare into the darkness, but we must be loved while we do. It is with this in mind that I remember the tremendous urge towards love in the harrowing story that is and was *Out the Window.*

Sarah Garton Stanley is a director, dramaturge, and conversationalist. She was the director of the Luminato production of Out the Window.

Production History
An *Out the Window* Chronology

2007: Solo Lab Cab Installation.

2008: The Theatre Centre Residency begins. (Incubation / investigation several times a year for a number of years.) Residency artists include Michelle Ramsay, Thomas Ryder Payne, and Trevor Schwellnus.

Rhubarb! Festival Showing, Buddies in Bad Times Theatre. Solo, plus one.

2009: Resident Artist at Crow's Theatre, dramaturgy and development.

2010: National Theatre School developmental workshop / Crow's Theatre, directed by Chris Abraham. Cast of 19.

2010: Workshop showing, The Theatre Centre / Crow's Theatre, directed by Chris Abraham. Cast of 8, including author.

2011: Works-in-Progress class at UWindsor / student investigation and new creation generated by OTW themes, text and transcripts.

2012: Free Fall workshop production / The Theatre Centre, directed by Liza Balkan. Cast of 7, plus audience participation.

2018: Luminato Festival inaugural partnership: The Theatre Centre / Luminato, directed by Sarah Garton Stanley. Cast of 10 plus audience engagement.

In between 2007 and 2012, developmental funding was received through the Ontario Arts Council, The Toronto Arts Council and The Canada Council for the Arts, The Theatre Centre as well as a number of private donors. Theatres that supported the project through OAC Recommender Grants included: Nightwood Theatre, Nightswimming, Factory Theatre, Theatre Passe Muraille, Crow's Theatre, and The Theatre Centre. In 2018, *Out the Window* was co-produced by the Luminato Festival and The Theatre Centre with performances at the Harbourfront Centre Theatre in Toronto.

Luminato Production

Out the Window was produced by The Luminato Festival and The Theatre Centre, June 19–24, 2018, Toronto, Ontario, Canada, with the following team:

Creative Team:

Liza Balkan	Creator and Writer*
Sarah Garton Stanley	Director
Tanisha Taitt	Associate Director
Trevor Schwellnus	Scenographer
Frank Donato	Design Coordinator
Ming Wong	Costumes
Nicholas Murray	Sound Designer
Sandy Plunkett	Stage Manager
Montgomery Martin	Networking Consultant
Kyle Purcell	Production and Promotional Photography

Cast:

Sarah Kitz	Liza
David Ferry	Lawyer 1
RH Thomson	Lawyer 2
Peyson Rock	Officer A / Waiter
Brett Donahue	Officer B / Waiter
Richard Lee	Officer C / Waiter
James Graham	Officer D / Waiter / Michael Vass

Live Artist	Syrus Marcus Ware
Musicians	LAL—Rosina Kazi and Nicholas Murray

Producing Team:

Sean Baker	Production Manager
Aislinn Rose	Producer and Creative Producer, The Theatre Centre
Franco Boni	General and Artistic Director, The Theatre Centre
Naomi Campbell	Deputy Artistic Director for Luminato
Josephine Ridge	Artistic Director of Luminato

*With Sarah Garton Stanley, Syrus Marcus Ware, Rosina Kazi, Nicholas Murray and the company.

Characters

LIZA: The witness. An actor and director. Open. Present. Honest. Funny. Responsive. Intelligent. No axe to grind. She inhales the abuse she receives in court and does her best to stay grounded through it all. Sometimes she fails at this. She is a novice witness, having only been on the stand in her past as a character on a TV series. Her mission: to offer her truth and to be a good witness, to continue to seek truth and eventually, to create a theatre project. The actor playing Liza should be mid–late 30s.

LAWYER 1: Defence lawyer. Male. Strong personality. He is a showman. Excellent at his job and knows it. One of the primary lawyers for police officers. Loves his own sense of humour and theatrics. Late 50s–mid 60s.

LAWYER 2: Prosecuting lawyer. Male. He is a down-to-earth, astute, human rights lawyer. The real deal. Works pro bono when he can. A mensch. Has a dry sense of humour. Believes in justice. Been around for a while. A grounded and good human being. Late 50s–mid 60s.

OFFICER A: Male. Late 20s–early 30s.

OFFICER B: Male. Late 20s–early 30s.

OFFICER C: Male. Early 30s.

OFFICER D: Male. Late 20s.

MICHAEL: Otto Vass's son. 18 years old. Played by the actor playing OFFICER D.

ARTIST

SINGER

Production Notes

This production is comprised of two parts, each informing the other:

Part One consists of two acts. It combines verbatim text from transcripts and interviews and includes a small portion of created text—material that has continued to be developed since 2007. It lives in the world of the protagonist's (Liza's) mind: potent memories and hauntings, and a step into the present. It is a highly theatrical world, filled with digital image and soundscape: scenes and visions zapping, lingering, surrounding, disappearing, and speeding forward.

Part Two is the third act. It was envisioned by director Sarah Garton Stanley, who guided its creation. This 45-minute act hurtles us right into the present. It offers a malleability that includes and embraces its particular audience, issues and locale. Its form is explained in greater detail in this script at the top of Part Two.

It has clear rules, yes, but it contains the messiness essential with being human. It is a conversation. It is a choir. It is a meal. It is an argument. It is an art gallery. It is a courtroom. It is a dance party. It is an honouring of Otto Vass and others who have lost their lives at the hands of the police.

Ultimately, to quote Sarah Garton Stanley, "the evening was created by a large company responding to the hesitancy we feel about our capacity, as urban dwellers, to effect change."

Part One tells a story. Part Two attempts to write a new one, with a centralizing question: "How to feel better." Under Sarah's profound leadership, we all dove into this question with daring, rigour, respect, and love.

I thank the members of our beautiful company for this extraordinary collaboration. I offer deep and continued gratitude to Franco Boni and The Theatre Centre for their unwavering support for this project over many years. I also want to express my heartfelt thanks to the Luminato Festival for choosing to produce it for its inaugural partnership with The Theatre Centre.

PART ONE

Syrus Marcus Ware drawing, Luminato production. Photo by Kyle Purcell.

Sarah Kitz as Liza. Photo by Kyle Purcell.

ACT I

SCENE 1

As the audience enters and takes their seats, the ARTIST is working on a large drawing on the floor in the middle of the playing area. The houselights are up. The space is open. The room belongs to all who inhabit it. The ARTIST is creating a larger-than-life-sized portrait of Otto Vass. At various points during Act 1, this work-in-progress is projected intermittently on the floor and walls. The sound of his work is amplified through a microphone attached to his wrist.

As the lights dim, music is heard, and the SINGER enters.

SINGER:
A gap
A space
An aperture
A crack
A crevice.
A hole
in recollection
You see that?
An opening
A breach
A blank to be filled in
You see that?
Oh—
Did you see that?
The gap is the sensate.
It is the careening adrenalin
Of time crashing still
While whipping forward

The gap contains the shock of the blow.
It holds the flesh of the flash of a moment

And its echoes.
Okay
Litigation demands the articulation of how
Something
Some one
Goes from being breath to being data.
How do you codify the coda of a heartbeat?
How do you codify the coda of a heartbeat.
How do you codify the coda of a heartbeat....

> *During the echo of the final lines the world begins to shift. We are now at the location of the incident. We soon see a woman (LIZA) looking out from her window on the top (5th) floor of a loft/apartment building.*

SIU INTERVIEWER:
9th of August 2000. The time's 0908 hours and this is Special Investigations Unit at College and Lansdowne in the city of Toronto. And we're investigating an incident that took place at this corner, in the early morning. Um, and with us is Ms. Lisa Balkan. ...Lisa—

LIZA:
(*From the window.*) Liza.

SIU:
(*Voiceover.*) Uh, Liza. I understand that uh you had some observations of what happened here this morning so maybe you could just basically explain what you saw.

> *OFFICERS enter. We see a shadowy re-enactment of the details being described below. During this, we see the following words on a screen:*

SCREEN:
All of the text you will hear in this story is 98.1% verbatim.

The rest is memory.

LIZA:
Sure. Um, I didn't see what happened I, uh, initially, um ... I first, I first heard yelling...A lot of yelling, I couldn't really figure out the key words and then I looked out my window. I'll now explain what I actually sa—I saw, uh, two

policemen, uh, beating up on him. Um, kicking him and hitting him with clubs. The, the sticks, I think at one point he must have been up. Then he was on the ground. Um, but the police proceed to beat him, punching him and in fact, uh, I saw him kicked in the groin I saw him kicked in the head and the whole body and, and beaten with the sticks.

SCREEN:
Memory is a cut-and-paste job.

LIZA:
I don't know how long that went on it went on—for several minutes—and the next thing was that two more police came. And he's a very, very big man and, and I didn't see any weapons on him. However, the other two joined in on, on beating. Um, again I don't know how long, a few minutes. Very, very fiercely. And my sense of it was that, maybe I'm projecting but they seemed to be so frustrated because he was so hard to subdue 'cause he's such a huge man and so angry or whatever. That their ire was elevated, and they just got angry themselves and just let it out. I yelled out "Stop" or whatever, but you know…

Memory is a cut-and-paste job. Photo by Kyle Purcell.

SIU:

About what time was this?

LIZA is now down on the ground near the action.

LIZA:

Oh, it was 12:15, 12:20, 12:30…time… (*Trails off.*)

Um, so after the four people beating on him, I think he was subdued, I didn't hear him anymore. More police cars came up. Um, the beating had stopped, there's no reason to continue, uh, uh, beating him. I had uh, uh, field glasses um, uh, what are they called? I remember seeing the backs of his legs. One leg crossed over the other, um, so I'm assuming they turned him over because the next time I looked he was on his back. Um, and I could see his face was very bloodied and, um, he was out. Fairly soon the cops were trying to do CPR on him. Eventually an ambulance arrived.

Police caution tape appears and surrounds the area.

They set up the yellow, the yellow uh, tick—yellow tape. They had the equipment for fib—fibulators—defibrillators. A lot of pumping on his chest and um, again a little mouth-to-mouth. But I have to say it went on a half hour to forty minutes. I figured that he was dead, just because the CPR was going on for much longer than anyone could sustain. Binoculars. That's the word I couldn't think of.

SIU:

And what do you do, miss?

LIZA:

Oh, I'm an actor…

SCREEN:
Huge applause signs fill the space, blinking at various speeds.

SOUND: *Applause.*

The caution tape disappears, as do the OFFICERS.

LIZA is alone on stage.

SCENE 2

OFFICERS A, B, C, and D are in a line, either in uniform or in civilian clothes. They speak in an easy, relaxed manner.

SCREEN:

August 9ᵗʰ, 2000:

Altercation between 4 police officers and a Mr. Vass.

The officers are charged with manslaughter.

OFFICER C:

Actually, I was toying with the idea of going into forensics or possibly becoming a pathologist... At 22, I decided to go to university. I obtained a Bachelor of Arts in sociology, with the majority of my courses being in criminology. I managed to obtain a job as a customs inspector over at the Ambassador Bridge, which is the major border crossing between Detroit, Michigan and Windsor, Ontario. That was more to gain some experience to get into the police service. I was 28 in 2000.

OFFICER D:

After graduating Grade 12, I took a two-year law and security course, which back then was a popular course to take for somebody that wanted to be a police officer. When I graduated from college I was only 19. At the time, you had to be 21. So, I—basically I worked for my father's construction company for a few years. When I graduated as a police officer I went to 14 Division. I was 27 at the time of the incident.

OFFICER A:

I was working towards a degree in psychology with a minor in sociology. But in my last semester unfortunately my parents split up. So, since my brother was out of the country attending school, it was obvious that I should go back home. And I took care of my mother for approximately two and a half years. Uh, I had experience volunteering in high school. Every couple of summers I volunteered with the physically / mentally, back then it was disabled, but I prefer challenged, but basically that gave me the background to get into a group home setting. These persons—I had occasion to take care of people suffering from schizophrenia, bipolar, mania, whatever they were referred to back then. In August 2000, I was 30 years old.

OFFICER B:
After I was done college I returned home. I worked in a factory. I was also a loss prevention officer at Zellers part-time. That's where I met my wife. (*Lightly.*) She wasn't stealing. She was working there. I was also a volunteer firefighter for about six months, the time it took to train me, and then I ran off to Toronto to be a police officer. The two things I always wanted to do. I was 28 in 2000.

SCENE 3

SCREEN:
Courtroom between 2002–2006

An image of court transcripts flashes onto the floor.

LIZA's manner on the stand is of someone who wants to do and say the right thing—to be a good, honest witness. She has no axe to grind.

COURT AUTHORITY:
(*Voiceover.*) You can sit down if you want or stand up, as you please.

LIZA:
I feel very short. I'll stand.

COURT AUTHORITY:
(*Voiceover.*) The other thing is that I'm going to ask you to make sure that you try to keep your voice up. It's a very large courtroom and there are a number of people in here.

LIZA:
Okay.

LAWYER 1
You "heard yelling outside."

LIZA nods yes.

LAWYER 1:
  You're nodding your head?

LIZA:
  Yes.

LAWYER 1:
  Where were you?

LIZA:
  In my kitchen.

LAWYER 1:
  Your kitchen.

LIZA:
  My whole apartment is my kitchen. It's a 600-square-foot loft, uh, room. One room.

LAWYER 1:
  Fair enough. What did you do when you heard yelling?

LIZA:
  I went over to the window that has a desk attached to it. I've got two sort of IKEA tables, that I put together that make up my desk—

LAWYER 1:
  Right—I prefer to ask my questions from stage left, to use your term.

LIZA:
  That would be stage right from my perspective.

LAWYER 1:
  From your perspective.

LIZA:
  From my perspective.

LAWYER 1:
  Ma'am, had you ever seen anything like this before?

LIZA:
  No. Not in—not in real life. No.

LAWYER 1:
In the movies you mean?

LIZA:
Movies, TV. Whatever.

LAWYER 1:
TV! So…it must have shocked you.

LIZA:
Yes, indeed.

LAWYER 1:
Now the beginning—well, you're in the acting business, right?

LIZA:
Yes, I am.

LAWYER 1:
And directing?

LIZA:
Yes.

LAWYER 1:
All right. Uh. Oh, are we talking about theatre, movies, or TV?

LIZA:
Primarily theatre.

LAWYER 1:
(*Clearly disappointed.*) Oh. Okay. So, you know then, as someone who directs others, if not acts in these things, that the beginning of these things is important, right?

LIZA:
Yes.

LAWYER 1:
Because it often explains why people do what they do?

LIZA:
Uh hmm.

LAWYER 1:
Is that right?

LIZA:
Yes…

LAWYER 1:
And if you're working with a bunch of actors about doing a scene, the motive for the characters in the scene is crucial to how you act in it, right?

LIZA:
Yes.

LAWYER 1:
In fact, that probably forms a large part of the discussion between the director and the actors, right?

LIZA:
Yes.

LAWYER 1:
Everybody gets together, and having read the script or the play or whatever, and says why are Dorothy and John behaving the way they are, right?

LIZA:
That would be correct. Have you acted?

LAWYER 1:
No. But I've seen a few act—actors, I mean. Let me just— let's back up a little. You "heard yelling outside."

LIZA nods.

LAWYER 1:
You're nodding your head?

LIZA:
Yes.

LAWYER 1:
You looked down at the scene from your window.

LIZA:
Yes.

LAWYER 1:
Right?

LIZA:
Yes.

LAWYER 1:
A considerable distance away, right?

LIZA:
I don't know how far it is.

LAWYER 1:
You have no idea.

LIZA:
I—no, I do not.

LAWYER 1:
Well, I think the police officer you did speak to—when he asked you to estimate the distance from your window to the scene, I think you told him that it was about a half a block, does that sound right?

LIZA:
I might have said that. (*Smiling.*) I've never been very good with distances, room sizes—

LAWYER 1:
So…half a block. How far is that?

LIZA:
Um … (*Lightly.*) It depends on the block…?

LAWYER 1:
(*Gently patronizing.*) All right. Now you've told the members of the jury that Mr. Vass was a very tall man.

LIZA:
Yes.

LAWYER 1:
And you've said on other occasions that he was a very large man. One of the descriptions you gave—you're nodding yes.

LIZA:
Yes, uh, I'm sorry. Yes.

LAWYER 1:
> And that you said that the first two officers on the scene would barely make up one of him. Is that right?

LIZA:
> Yes, I said that.

LAWYER 1:
> Would it surprise you to learn that Mr. Vass, at least according to the evidence that we are going to hear from the pathologist, was at most between 5 foot 3 and 5 foot 4 inches?

ON SCREEN:
Exhibit A: an animation of the corner where the incident took place. This image soon expands and fills the entire playing space.

LAWYER 1:
> You don't know why these parties were fighting?

LIZA:
> No, I don't.

LAWYER 1:
> You don't know who attacked who?

LIZA:
> No. I did not see that. No.

LAWYER 1:
> How many times did you think you looked away from this thing?

LIZA:
> I'd be guessing. I don't remember.

LAWYER 1:
> Okay. But it was several times, right?

LIZA:
> A few times.

LAWYER 1:
> Okay… And the reason you had to was why?

LIZA:

Because I realized subconsciously at the moment that I was a witness to something and it was important for me to keep watching.

LAWYER 1:

So, you were actually articulating that to yourself, since you were the only person there?

LIZA:

Probably.

LAWYER 1:

You were actually having a chat with your subconscious?

LIZA:

I live alone. I talk to myself. Yes.

LAWYER 1:

Uh hmmm. But with your self-conscious though—subconscious, I mean?

LIZA:

(*Laughing,*) Years of therapy. I don't know what to tell you.

LAWYER 1:

Therapy? I don't mean to imply—

LIZA:

(*Lightly with understated humour.*) Look, I lived in New York for many years. I didn't know anyone who wasn't in therapy.

LAWYER 1:

I just want to make sure that I'm talking to one of you and not two of you.

> *Pause. A shift of some kind. The air changes in the room. An internal moment for LIZA. She begins to physically/ mentally re-enact the moment below as she continues the testimony.*

LIZA:

I came home, took off my party clothes, made myself a cup of tea and then I heard...

LAWYER 1:
I was asking about how you missed the beginning,

LIZA:
Um hmm.

LAWYER 1:
On the basis of what you saw while you were watching, did you—did you form the opinion that Mr. Vass was defending himself or attacking the police?

LIZA's attention returns to the court.

LIZA:
Defending himself.

LAWYER 1:
All right. And what was the basis for that opinion?

LIZA:
He had no weapons on him. He had nothing on except his clothes. The only kicking and beating that I saw was coming from the officers.

LAWYER 1:
So, if I get this right, based on what you saw, these officers, for no good reason that you could see, were simply attacking him, do I have that right?

LIZA:
I saw the officers attacking him.

LAWYER 1:
And for no good reason that you could see?

LIZA:
That term "for no good reason." I did not see what happened prior to that.

LAWYER 1:
Well, Okay. So, it stands to reason then that if he'd attacked them, they would be defending themselves and that would be a reason, wouldn't it?

LIZA:
That's possible. That's not what I saw.

LAWYER 1:

Well, except that—except that precisely, it's because you didn't see the beginning that you can't answer the question adequately, isn't that right?

LIZA:

I didn't see the beginning.

LAWYER 1:

Well, I understand that but... Have you ever rented a movie and run it fast forward and then begun after the first 20 minutes?

LIZA:

Actually yes, but in this case...

LAWYER 1:

You have?

LIZA:

Yes, I have but in this case it's irrelevant.

LAWYER 1:

But you wouldn't recommend it as a policy...

LIZA:

No.

LAWYER 1:

...to comprehend a film, would you?

LIZA:

No.

LAWYER 1:

Or show up late at the theatre and miss the first act, especially if you were directing it?

LIZA:

No.

LAWYER 1:

I mean...did you ever see that Woody Allen movie called *Annie Hall*?

LIZA:

Yes.

LAWYER 1:

And do you remember that scene where he goes on a date with Diane Keaton and he takes her to that repertory theatre and he goes up to the box office to buy tickets and he comes back and says, "We can't go in"? Do you remember that scene?

LIZA:

I remember them seeing *The Sorrow and the Pity*, but that's all I remember.

LAWYER 1:

You remember them what, sorry....

LIZA:

I remember them seeing the film *The Sorrow and the Pity* but that's all I remember.

LAWYER 1:

Well, as I remember it…

SCENE 4

SOUND: At the movies. Clarinet music is heard underneath the following dialogue.

VIDEO: Starscape.

FLOOR PROJECTORS: Beams like film premiere searchlights.

LAWYER 1:

He's a director like you're a director; he comes over to her and he says, "We can't go in."

And she says, "Why?"

And he says, "'Cause we're seven minutes late. It's already begun."

And she says, "Well, how many times have you seen this movie?"

And he says, "30." But they don't go in.

The music and lights stop as LAWYER 2 rises.

SCENE 5

An image of court transcripts flashes onto the floor.

LAWYER 2:

I'm going to rise at this point, Your Honour.

Amusing as my colleague's recollections of Diane Keaton's role in Woody Allen's *Annie Hall* are, firstly, they're not relevant; secondly, she has no recollection of the scene. There's no purpose, except for the purposes of argument, in asking the question, which my friend was doing. Where my friend is leading with this line of questions is to ask the witness to interpret what happened. Her role here is to tell us what she saw and what she did. It's not for the witness to interpret. It's for the jury to interpret—and in my submission, this kind of questioning is not proper!

Beat.

LAWYER 1:

You were going to say it's really hard to remain neutral in these events.

LIZA:

No, no, in fact, I wasn't.

LAWYER 1:

That's of course what happened to you in August 2000. You plugged into the "Justice for Otto Vass" website and that really had a huge impact on your views of the whole thing from then on.

LIZA:

It didn't have a huge impact.

LAWYER 1:

Ms. Balkan, it's only after you looked at the Otto Vass website that you decided to march, I'm gonna put it, in solidarity with these folks.

LIZA:

I never even turned on my computer. If I saw that the rally was happening downstairs, I would have joined it because I needed to be a part of something.

LAWYER 1:
  Join the Y.

LIZA:
  I already have.

LAWYER 2:
  Well, Your Honour, to me, that's just sarcasm.

LAWYER 1:
  Well, I wasn't being—

LAWYER 2:
  Regardless of the benefits of joining the Y, it's neither relevant or appropriate. It was sarcasm pure and simple.

LAWYER 1:
  I wasn't trying to be sarcastic.

LAWYER 2:
  (*To LIZA.*) I apologize. My friend was being sarcastic.

LAWYER 1:
  But surely my friend can see a concern about—about her tendency to do exactly that. To interpret, to fill in gaps. She's marching in a demonstration, which doesn't believe in the presumption of innocence.

LIZA:
  Yes, but…

LAWYER 1:
  Thirdly, you're speaking to people at the scene who have their own perspectives on what did or didn't happen and whether they're eyewitnesses or not eyewitnesses. Fourth, you're reading all the, or many of the media accounts about the case. Fifth…

LIZA:
  …Uh….

LAWYER 1:
  Now it sounds like you went up to a cameraperson and said, "You know I think I'm a witness here and no one really wants to talk to me." Did you say that?

LIZA:
Those are the words I used, yes.

LAWYER 1:
Okay. Was it about you getting on television as opposed to the event?

LIZA:
Oh no, no, not at all.

LAWYER 1:
No?

LIZA:
I felt that as a witness to this event that it should be heard.

LAWYER 1:
Was it your expectation that the moment that you walked out someone would say, "There is Lisa Balkan. She was a witness. I want to interview her"? Is that what you were thinking?

LIZA:
No.

LAWYER 1:
I mean you weren't trying to make the story Lisa Balkan's participation in it?

LIZA:
It's Liza.

> Beat.

LAWYER 1:
"Liza."

LIZA:
Sorry— (*For being rude.*)

LAWYER 1:
Sorry— (*For mispronouncing.*)

LIZA:
Sorry...

LAWYER 1:
Sorry...

LIZA:

(*Beat.*) What I would say is that I was very aware of seeing four people hitting one person who was, at that point, from the time there were four people, he was on the ground... I can't tell you who... I can't—

LAWYER 1:

So your impression that four people—

LIZA:

That is what I saw. That's what I told the SIU. That's my version of what I saw.

LAWYER 1:

Your version.

LIZA:

That is the truth of what I saw. Otherwise I wouldn't have said it.

LAWYER 1:

That's what you honestly believe?

LIZA:

Yes.

LAWYER 1:

That that's your impression?

LIZA:

In that everything in life is an impression. Yes.

COURT AUTHORITY:

(*Voiceover.*) Witness, I'm just going to ask you to step out for a moment, please...

> *LIZA "exits." We see her trying to regroup and stay grounded as she walks around the perimeter during the following.*

SCENE 6

We are still in the courtroom.

LAWYER 1:

I'm entitled to ask the witness to restrict herself to what it is she remembers standing here today in the courtroom. I can't cross-examine two people simultaneously on two separate accounts, one given on the night, and one given here today. I'm entitled to her evidence here today under oath and cross-examined under oath.

LAWYER 2:

The witness, in response to a series of questions, had indicated that in an earlier statement to the Special Investigations Unit, she made certain assertions. While she may not have a full recollection today of what is asserted in that statement, she stands by it as being accurate. In essence what she is articulating is the doctrine of past recollection recorded, which is relatively simple and recognizes that human memories can fade.

SCENE 7

A time jump but...we are still in the courtroom.

LIZA:

I was above the parking lot of 7-Eleven, Harvey's...lots of sky. I can see east and west as well... I mean, it's where College and Dundas almost kiss, so there are streetcar tracks every which way; that bridge heading towards Roncesvalles (with a sharp incline on either end that's a pain in the ass if you're biking...)

Then LIZA is enveloped by a projection of a 3D modelling of the actual corner. The street corner, building, windows and parking lot, the Tim Hortons, pizza place, store, sky.

A remembering writ large.

LIZA:

Mr. Vass owned a shop across the way—used furniture and junk that cascaded out onto the corner. Old toasters, lamps, stereo equipment...maybe...

The 7-Eleven is now an S Market. But it's open 24 hours, so that's okay. The Harvey's is now a Tim Hortons... It's almost like it didn't happen. But a pizza place is still there so... (*Unspoken: It did.*) The parking lot's been repaved...

SCENE 8

A time jump. Still in the courtroom. OFFICERS A and B testify. LIZA watches.

An image of court transcripts flashes onto the floor.

LAWYER 1:

I'm going to ask you now to take your mind back to that particular incident now. You receive an "unwanted guest" call on the dispatch. You arrive in the vicinity of the 7-Eleven location.

OFFICER B:

We approached Mr. Vass when we entered the store. We asked Mr. Vass something along the lines of, "Do you want to come outside with us?" Mr. Vass seemed cooperative, he seemed fine with that.

OFFICER A:

He seemed a little disoriented. His clothing was dishevelled. I remember you could see his stomach and he had shorts on. Initial reaction, I don't like to judge people, but my gut feeling is that this person might be a homeless person or someone who just got into a fight.

LAWYER 1:

This is all still inside the store, right?

OFFICER A:

Still in the store, yes.

LAWYER 1:

Okay.

OFFICER A:

I propped the door open. And then Mr. Vass, myself, and my partner exit the store. It was my understanding, or my belief, at that time, that this person might have been a victim or involved in some kind of—I recollect he might have said something in the store that he was assaulted or something.

OFFICER B:

It was my understanding, yes, before we were dispatched, that he was in a fight, yes.

LAWYER 2:

I would put it to you sir, the first thing that you would do is ask him, "Where did those guys go?" Because they might still be in the neighbourhood, right?

OFFICER B:

You could suggest that. That's not what I did.

LAWYER 2:

That's not what you did. I'm doubting your evidence, sir. I'm suggesting to you, sir, that if you were telling the truth, obviously the first thing that you would have to do, as a half-way intelligent police officer in that circumstance, is say: "Where did they go?" Because they might be right down the street and this is your last chance to get them, isn't that fair?

OFFICER B:

I guess that's why I'm a police officer and you are a lawyer.

I asked Mr. Vass to produce some identification. He pulled a wallet out of his back pocket.

LAWYER 1:

Okay.

OFFICER B:

He started fumbling through it. He then put his wallet back in his pocket without giving me anything. At that point, I asked Mr. Vass again if he could provide me some identification. He again pulled his wallet out of his back pocket. He sort of fumbled through it. At this time, I assisted him and said that the health card would be fine.

LAWYER 2:

He twice asked for his ID back after he gave it to you, you said both times, "Wait a minute. I'm getting the information," or words to that effect?

OFFICER B:
I asked him if he could wait a minute.

LAWYER 2:
But evidently, he didn't feel he could because he asked you again, right?

OFFICER B:
Yes.

LAWYER 2:
So now you have a situation. You have somebody you consider to be a victim of a crime—

OFFICER B:
Yes.

LAWYER 2:
—who started to talk to you about it and gave you identification but then said he wanted to discuss it in a police station, and you said no.

OFFICER B:
That's correct.

LAWYER 1:
What happened next?

OFFICER B:
He lunged forward and punched me in the, on my left side with his right fist. My partner, who was standing beside him, grabbed him sort of from behind into a bear hug. He was still swinging his arms, but he was still coming towards me. I went forward, and I grabbed Mr. Vass's shirt. I advised: "You're under arrest for assaulting police." And I said, "Get down on the ground." I pushed forward.

OFFICER A:
The next thing I know I'm on my back, knocked silly.

LAWYER 1:
Sorry, knocked...?

OFFICER A:
Knocked silly, for lack of a better word.

OFFICER B:

I don't know how, but we all fell down. My partner landed on his back. Mr. Vass landed on my partner, and I landed on Mr. Vass.

OFFICER A:

I just landed on my head—right on the cement with my head, and I was semi-unconscious.

LAWYER 1:

Okay. So your next sort of awareness after being sort of struck or landing on the ground was what?

OFFICER A:

I was lying there stunned and was kind of messed up. And then I believe it was the back of his head, I'm assuming, hit me in the forehead, because he was lying right in front of me. It kind of woke me up, and I realized that I was in a situation here that I had to control or try to control.

OFFICER B:

I don't know how my partner got from underneath him, but he did. Mr. Vass was now on his back on the pavement. He was whaling about and punching still. And he started kicking in a sort of—bicycle-kicking motion. He was kneeing me in the back as I was on his—I was on his right side trying to control his right arm. And the reason I was trying to control his right arm was to put a handcuff on it and to arrest him.

LAWYER 1:

Do you recall whether either Mr. Vass or your partner said anything at that point?

OFFICER A:

I heard my partner, I believe, yelling, "Stop resisting, stop resisting." Mr. Vass at this point I think was yelling, but because I was so close to him it didn't make sense to me. I was trying to make sense of the situation.

OFFICER B:

At no time during the entire incident did Mr. Vass stop resisting.

LAWYER 1:

(*To OFFICER A.*) All right. I appreciate things are happening kind of quickly at this point, but just to summarize: Your objective at that point was simply to try to keep this gentleman on the ground.

OFFICER A:

Oh, entirely. Like he's—we're trained that a person is less of a threat if they are on the ground.

The testimony shifts and spins from one officer to the other with increasing frenzy.

OFFICER B:

Mr. Vass, he—he seemed like he had this superhuman strength. He put his right foot in my stomach and he kicked me. I was in the air. He's going ballistic.

OFFICER A:

He was elbowing me—he's spitting. His head is flying around.

Courtroom. "I was trying to make sense of the situation." Photo by Kyle Purcell.

OFFICER B:
I knew that Mr. Vass was a lot stronger than we were.

OFFICER A:
He's going crazy.

OFFICER B:
So I had a police radio and I asked for more units please.

OFFICER A:
His eyes going wild.

OFFICER B:
I kept on trying to grab his arm.

OFFICER A:
He's going crazy.

OFFICER B:
He kept on breaking free from my grasp.

OFFICER A:
It scared me.

OFFICER B:
He kept on hitting me.

OFFICER A:
He's going crazy.

OFFICER B:
I kept on yelling, "Stop resisting, stop resisting."

OFFICER A:
He's like an—

OFFICER B:
He was still kneeing and kicking me.

The frenzy stops.

OFFICER A:
He's like an—I don't want to call him an animal. Obviously, he isn't. It's just animalistic rage. So basically, when he would lash out and hit my body, I gave him a distractionary technique to the face to kind of distract him. It's like an open-hand technique, and I gave him a

slight, little jab to his mouth. Every time that he lashed out or hit me or a knee came close to my head, I would give him a distractionary technique to the mouth as if to distract him.

OFFICER B:

At that point, for my safety I decided to stand up and I took out my ASP out of its holster. As Mr. Vass was kicking out at me I'd hit him on the leg with the ASP. I did that about six or seven times as he was kicking out towards me. I was hoping to get some sort of pain compliance. It's not nice but the ASP is meant to hurt someone.

LAWYER 1:

Go on.

OFFICER B:

At that point, I turn around and I saw my partner on his knees on Mr. Vass's left side and I saw Mr. Vass's left hand in the area of my partner's gun. I can't say specifically if it was on the gun, but it was definitely in the area of the holster. I was thinking the only reason he was doing this was because he wanted to kill us. He made that clear because he said, "I'll kill you." Or something to that effect. At that point, fearing for my partner's and my safety, I ran toward Mr. Vass and I kicked twice as hard as I could in the left upper thigh.

SCENE 9

A time jump. Still in the courtroom.

An image of court transcripts flashes onto the floor.

LAWYER 2:

Once you're using a baton, you're not trying to just poke somebody or something like that. If you're swinging a baton, you're swinging to get maximum effect from that baton, right?

OFFICER B:

That's correct.

LAWYER 2:
And that's the training, to swing as hard as you can, right?

OFFICER B:
Yes.

LAWYER 2:
And that's what you did on this occasion, right?

OFFICER B:
Yes, it is.

LAWYER 2:
Yes. Now, sir, do you have the ASP with you, please.

OFFICER B:
I do not. I believe Constable—

The ARTIST offers up a baton to OFFICER B.

LAWYER 2:
Sir, I would request that you open it once again. And I would request that we all watch the opening.

OFFICER B expands the baton.

Officer B (Brett Donohue) with the ASP (baton). Photo by Kyle Purcell.

LAWYER 2:
>So it's a flick. And then how did you use it on Mr. Vass's legs that night? Try to illustrate, make-believe without connecting with anything.

OFFICER B:
>We—

LAWYER 2:
>Perhaps you want to stand in front here, so we can all see you very clearly.

OFFICER B:
>We are trained to hit from overhead, like that.

>>*OFFICER B demonstrates.*

LAWYER 2:
>And you'd be swinging as hard as you could each time.

OFFICER B:
>Yes. We're actually trained to hit like this, and come down like that again. I was hitting just like this.

>>*OFFICER B demonstrates again.*

LAWYER 2:
>So you weren't doing any backhands this time. You were just doing forward. I'd like to have the jury look at this and consider what this does as it's swung as hard as this officer can. Could you do it just a couple of more times, please? That's only one, okay.

>>*OFFICER B swings harder a few more times.*

>>*Then:*

SCENE 10

>*We are back at the moment of Vass's death.*

>*OFFICERS A, B, C, and D are in the fray with an invisible Vass. They are re-enacting according to their perspective as it is being stated in the courtroom.*

>*LIZA watches as though she is back in her apartment.*

OFFICER D:

I show up, I do a circle around him, reach over and grab his left hand.

OFFICER B:

I remember seeing lights from behind me from a car, then I remember seeing out of my peripheral vision two police officers running...

OFFICER D:

The whole intention here is to get him flipped over and handcuffed. It wasn't easy. The position I was in—it was like if you picture someone pulling rope, like a tug of war. You've got your foot planted and you're kind of pulling and leaning back.

OFFICER C:

I go from being a witness within a split second to being a participant in this event.

OFFICER B:

At that point, Mr. Vass was still moving. He's still kicking. I believe my partner went to his feet to stop his feet from kicking.

OFFICER B:

I asked everyone if they were okay.

OFFICER A:

Everyone seemed to be fine.

OFFICER C:

To my right Constable B slipped the handcuff onto the right wrist.

OFFICER B:

My concern was his legs because I had hit him on the legs with the ASP.

OFFICER A:

Mr. Vass was on his stomach for a very, very short time, like five seconds. I rolled him over to his right side, still handcuffed.

OFFICER B:
I rolled him over onto his side.

OFFICER A:
And officers kept on coming.

LIZA is agitated.

LIZA:
Call 911...

OFFICER B:
I saw that he was purplish-blue. I yelled that he wasn't breathing. We immediately rolled him onto his stomach, removed one handcuff from one wrist, rolled him back onto his back and then removed the other handcuff from his other wrist.

OFFICER A:
And officers kept on coming.

OFFICER B:
(*He refers to Officers C and D.*) They started CPR right away.

LIZA:
I kept thinking: Call 911.

OFFICER A:
I'm praying to God like, "Why is this happening?" And I just wanted to help Mr. Vass. I'm not going to stop pushing on his chest until—and I just remember every part of my body was on fire and I was just praying to God. I wanted this person to wake up.

LIZA:
Call 911.

OFFICER B:
CPR was done from the moment we noticed he wasn't breathing, right until the ambulance arrived, from what I understand, 45 minutes later.

LIZA:
But, you know—they were already there.

The SINGER crosses upstage, singing:

SINGER:
Did you see that? Did you see that?

SCENE 11

Scene of the Event

THE OFFICERS realize that Vass is dead and back away.

We focus in on the sound of the ARTIST's work and project some element of the work on the screen.

SCENE 12

The OFFICERS are up on the mezzanine level of the theatre.

OFFICER A:
I was driven back to 14th Division and placed in our secretary's office.

OFFICER D is breathing, catching his breath. This continues through the dialogue below.

OFFICER C:
Apparently, someone put me in their car and took me back to the station.

OFFICER B:
We were separated. I was driven by a young officer. He was so new. In fact, I remember him asking for directions…

Sound of OFFICER D breathing.

OFFICER A:
From what I remember, they had an officer from another division guard the hallway in between various office doors that we were in. Basically, his job was to ensure that there was no communication between the four of us.

OFFICER C:
They lock you in a room for three or four hours by yourself…

Sound of OFFICER D breathing.

OFFICER A:
Around 5 o'clock in the morning, shortly after my uniform was seized, I got in my car and I drove home.

LIZA and OFFICER C have a moment of connection. Silence.

OFFICER C:
And that's when you realize you're never going to be the same again.

SCENE 13

We are back in the courtroom.

An image of court transcripts flashes onto the floor.

LAWYER 1:
Up to the point where the two officers—the second set—arrive, I'm going to suggest that what you saw was a struggle, a battle going on among the three of them.

LIZA:
It never seemed like that to me when I was watching. It didn't seem like a battle.

LAWYER 1:
Okay. Do you recollect ever describing it as such?

LIZA:
It's possible I used those words. Did I? You have them.

LAWYER 1:
Let me—but again, you know the difference between, say, a beating and a battle. Right? I mean they're different words for a reason. Right?

LIZA:
Yes.

LAWYER 1:
I mean a battle is different than, say, a fight is different than a beating.

LIZA:

Yes. I would say that with a battle you have two opposing teams, and even though it initially seemed like—I wasn't sure if he was lashing out at them or trying to defend himself.

LAWYER 1:

I understand. And of course, the reason you were in the dark is because you literally were in the dark about that?

LIZA:

What do you mean?

LAWYER 1:

As in, you weren't down there.

LIZA:

I will say that I'm very sure of what I saw.

LAWYER 1:

You said you saw Mr. Vass kicked in the head.

LIZA:

He was kicked all over.

LAWYER 1:

In the head?

LIZA:

Well, he must have been because his face was all bloodied.

LAWYER 1:

And so are you guessing?

LIZA:

I would say yes.

LAWYER 1:

You were guessing, or you saw him kicked in the head?

LIZA:

That I saw him.

LAWYER 1:

Did you see him kicked in the head?

LIZA:

I don't remember.

LAWYER 1:
You're not sure. Right?

LIZA:
No.

LAWYER 1:
At the preliminary inquiry you said—

"There, uh, there were times when, perhaps I couldn't see his face because there were—there were times when there were bodies over him in the battle, in the fight, whatever, so I couldn't always clearly see his face."

So do you agree you gave that answer to that question?

LIZA:
(*Tears up.*) If I may, pardon me, Mr.— Pardon me. I think the battle I was referring to was seeing four people fighting with—hitting someone who was down on the ground. So it's a form of battle, but it's not what I would call—

An OFFICER offers LIZA a tissue.

LIZA:
(*To the OFFICER.*) Thank you very much. Pardon me.

LIZA:
(*To LAWYER 1.*) I think there's a difference between the type of battle I think you might be meaning and what I'm trying to convey here.

LAWYER 1:
Well, I'm just confirming that, in fact, those were the two words you used. "Battle" and "fight."

LIZA:
Yes.

LAWYER 1:
You described him as someone who has lots of energy and who was very angry.

LIZA:
Yes.

LAWYER 1:
In fact, when you were first interviewed by the SIU you said that he, Mr. Vass, was fighting a bit. You agree?

LIZA:
If I said those words, it seems like, then initially, it was hard for me to figure out.

LAWYER 1:
Really?

LIZA:
Yes, he may have been fighting back at first.

LAWYER 1:
Yes?

LIZA:
But that was only—that was only for a short time, because he was really starting—I mean they had him on the ground and he was yelling and maybe kicking, trying to fight them off.

LAWYER 1:
When the matter was going on and you were looking at it, there's no question you were in an emotional state. Right?

LIZA:
It was a difficult thing to watch.

LAWYER 1:
I mean you got emotional about it just here today.

LIZA says nothing.

LAWYER 1:
Do you imagine that your emotions then coloured your view of what happened?

LIZA:
Honestly, no.

LAWYER 1:
You described it as a murder.

LIZA:
Did I use those words?

LAWYER 1:
Yes.

LIZA:
Then kill, murdered, yes.

LAWYER 1:
Murdered. There's a big difference, isn't there?

LIZA:
If someone kills someone, if someone murders someone.

LAWYER 1:
In your mind, they're the same?

LIZA:
I suppose murder sounds harsher. I know I used both those terms.

LAWYER 1:
Okay. So, certainly, within a month of this event when you sat down with an inspector and said this, I suggest, you had made up your mind, lost all your objectivity. Right?

LIZA:
I had made up my mind in terms of what I know I saw. I saw this altercation and I saw someone killed.

LAWYER 1:
Yeah.

LIZA:
To my mind.

LAWYER 1:
No, murdered. That's the word you used.

LIZA:
That's one of the words I used.

LAWYER 1:
Let's be precise here. You believe—at least within a month after the event—that the officers sitting over here murdered Mr. Vass before your very eyes. Right?

LIZA:
That's…what it looked like to me.

LAWYER 1:
And within that month, what we also know is you still did not know how it began.

LIZA:
That's true.

LAWYER 1:
And still don't.

LIZA:
Uh, I read some accounts, but you know—

LAWYER 1:
Those accounts including "The Committee for Justice for Otto Vass" website, right?

LIZA:
Initially, I wanted to get as much information about what was being said from everywhere.

LAWYER 1:
Sure. You looked at the photos of Mr. Vass's injuries that were put up on the internet. They "swamped your mind," as you said.

LIZA:
(*Offering herself to the lions.*) Did I say those words?

LAWYER 1:
Yes.

LIZA:
Oh fine, yes.

LAWYER 1:
Tell the jury what it means.

LIZA:
I guess there were so many awful pictures in my head from having seen it first-hand and then continuing to see it in the papers and yes, online and whatever the website is.

LAWYER 1:
You have to admit, you exhibited a great deal of uncertainty as to what you saw.

LIZA:
(*Losing steam.*) I wasn't clear on who was doing what.

LAWYER 1:
You use phrases: "I saw badges, then I guess I didn't see badges, well perhaps I'm thinking of too much TV; perhaps I placed a shirt on him in my memory, uh, I actually feel like I'm making that up now; I don't remember; I seem to remember." You use that phrase often, "I seem to remember." Is that just a figment of speech or... does "I seem to remember" mean you are uncertain—

LIZA:
Uh—

LAWYER 1:
"—It's possible I'm trying to put something together right now; there might have been one of them using a baton," then you go "There might have been two more." You don't know that there were four but it's possible... "I'm trying to think if I heard his 'Get away'" or whatever, or whether you were just guessing about that... And what I'm gonna suggest is that there's a common theme: One of the things you do, with great respect, is that where there are gaps in recollection, you fill them in. You see that?

LIZA:
—

LAWYER 1:
And you agree objectivity is like fairness?

LIZA:
Yes.

LAWYER 1:
And that fairness and objectivity depend on a full and accurate picture of what occurred before one makes up his or her mind.

LIZA:
Yes.

LAWYER 1:
And I thought you agreed with me that that was good common sense. Okay. So can you tell—help the jury with an idea of, during this period, at what point you ceased to be objective about this event?

LIZA is left alone. Vulnerable. Destroyed.

Beat.

SCENE 14

THE SINGER sings. LIZA stands alone, her face projected large on the screen. She is open, raw; breathing in her present, even as the present shifts into the future of the following act. This is a transition wherein past, present and future become one.

Cross-examination. Alone on the witness stand. Sarah Kitz as Liza. Photo by Kyle Purcell.

SINGER:
a gap
a space
an aperture
A crack
A crevice.
A hole
in recollection
You see that?
The gap is the sensate.
It's the careening adrenalin
Of time crashing still
As it whips forward

The gap is filled with savage scenery
(It is) The view when lying on the pavement
Looking up while being pummelled,
(It is) The view when looking down as your foot kicks his face
(It is) The landscape from the railing on the porch across the way
(It is) The air, five flights above
between my hands on the glass and the parking lot below.
It is both crystalline and incoherent all at once.

I remember him standing. I remember him sitting with his legs out.
I remember jumping back.
You see that?
Oh
You see that.

The landscape of the gap is jagged terrain
it is prehistoric.
We're talking tectonic plates here.
But boundaries between plates are often ill-defined.

They are hidden beneath the oceans

Hidden beneath emotions
Eroding upon contact.
Dissolving in the very moment of translation.

The gap is the sensate.
The careening adrenalin
Of time crashing still
As it whips forward

> *During the song: LIZA is helped into a change of costume, while still standing on stage, visible to all.*
>
> *A table and three chairs appear. Two waiters' side stations are set in the space.*
>
> *The WAITERS are at the ready with water to fill glasses, etc. They are in white shirts, black ties, short black aprons: upscale wait staff uniform.*
>
> *The LAWYERS have changed their clothes.*

ACT II

SCENE 1

A restaurant on St. Clair West in Toronto.

SCREEN:
2010: A restaurant uptown.

LIZA and LAWYER 2 are in mid-conversation. A small cassette recorder/dictaphone is on the table. WAITERS hover in the background.

LIZA:
I wouldn't let my mother sit in the audience during the prelim. Or trial. It wouldn't have been helpful to witness her anxiety while I was on the stand. I did ask some—some theatre friends—artists—to come. I figured that if things got rocky for me up there I'd look out at them and get grounded. You know?

> *Beat.*

My mother did come to my installation in '07 and...she saw the 25-minute workshop thing that I did in '08—

LAWYER 2:
At that theatre downtown. Right.

LIZA:
Right. So glad you came to that. I really hoped I wouldn't get sued.

LAWYER 2:
You know, if you get sued by the Police Association, it would be good in a way in that it would highlight the politics of the case. You have a right to express your opinion. In my view the arts in Canada are very timid. (*Beat.*) I'll be curious to see what you make of me in your next version. (*Laughing.*) But I won't sue you for libel.

Beat.

LIZA:

Thanks for helping to organize this.

> *LIZA fast-forwards the tape. The action in the restaurant occurs in triple time.*

> *LAWYER 2 enters and sits, orders from the menu. LIZA stops the tape and the action resumes at normal speed.*

LAWYER 2:

Look, in my view, it's a myth that people are neutral. Nobody is neutral. Especially about police interactions. Why do we get nervous when we see a police officer? (*Beat.*) You know, you might want to think about getting in touch with the force...

LAWYER 1:

It's not gonna happen.

LIZA:

I mean I could just phone up a division and ask them...

LAWYER 1:

Their answer is gonna be no.

> *LAWYER 2 silently agrees.*

> *LIZA fast-forwards the tape recorder. Waiters serve food in triple time etc.*

> *She stops the tape.*

SCENE 2

LAWYER 1:

(*To the WAITER.*) Thanks, buddy.

But anyway, the trial did give rise to one of the great all-time anecdotes. And that was our discussion about Woody Allen's *Annie Hall*.

LIZA:

I was going to ask you— (*About that.*)

LAWYER 1:

I have to admit that I'm really grateful I didn't listen to the voice over my shoulder that said, "Don't do it..." Because it was one of the more effective pieces of cross-examination that I've ever used. Because the jury loved it. And so did His Honour. And you were kind enough to agree that missing the beginning—even in the courtroom—was significant to your ability to figure out what the hell had happened.

LIZA:

I don't think I actually said that—

LAWYER 1:

Oh, yeah.

LIZA:

But, interesting.

LAWYER 1:

I think that's what everybody in the room thought.

LIZA:

Yeah, well... *(Laughs.)*

LAWYER 1:

So, all I had to do was push the button and that issue was now on the table. I was real tentative about using it. I thought: "Do I, do I? Uhh..." I thought: I don't want to trivialize things, it's early in the trial... I think you were like the third witness maybe and uh, I didn't want the jury to get the kooky idea that I was kinda being a card... and I didn't know how the judge was going to respond because I'd only ever done really small stuff in front of him and it was my first big show with him and you know, he did Bernardo... And the room was full of the press and whatever, whatever...

LIZA:

Yes.

LAWYER 1:

...and then, when I finished, I looked over at His Honour, I could see, you know: "Nice job...."

LIZA:
Tape Change.

> *LIZA stops the tape. THE LAWYERS appear to continue talking, possibly saying things that LIZA would really want to capture for transcript. She fumbles in her bag: Where is the tape?? She really wants to record what is being said... Eventually she finds it, struggles with changing and replacing the cassette tape and places the cassette recorder back on the table with gusto. The lawyers stop talking and just smile benignly at the nice meal they are having.*

> *LIZA starts the tape.*

LAWYER 1:
People are always telling me I should write about the stuff I've done, and I don't discourage them, I've just not gotten around to it. I have no doubt it would be interesting.

Tape change. Sarah Kitz, RH Thompson, David Ferry. Background: Richard Lee, James Graham, Peyson Rock, Brett Donohue. Photo by Kyle Purcell.

This isn't what LIZA wants to recall. LIZA stops the tape and fast-forwards.

SCENE 3

Later in the restaurant.

Laughter. The WAITERS re-enter and serve.

LAWYER 2:
A guy walked around Edward's Gardens acting strangely. Wanna pass the pepper? He's walking around with a big knife. The police are called. Justifiably. Understandably.

Simultaneously:

LAWYER 1:
Yeah.

LIZA:
Yeah.

LAWYER 2:
The police come and they confront him. He doesn't have the knife on him and they don't say, "Excuse me, sir, can we have a word with you...?" Keep things cool. They say, "GET DOWN on the ground." The guy says—and he has mental health problems—he says quite rationally, "What for?" And as far as he was concerned, he wasn't doing anything. He was wandering around in the park. And they don't answer him, they wrestle him down on the ground. "FIRST WE TAKE CONTROL." He breaks away, he runs away, they end up killing him. Shooting him.

LAWYER 1:
I've never met a police officer who shot a guy who didn't feel like he had to. What I find is an unbelievable amount of reserve on their part.

Anyway, I'm surprised it happens as rarely as it does.

LIZA:
Uh, but—

LAWYER 1:
This takes us to Otto Vass, of course, 'cause you know, but for his mental illness he would be here.

LIZA stops the tape. Rewind. Stop. Play.

Anyway, I'm surprised it happens as rarely as it does.

LIZA:
Uh, but—

LAWYER 1:
This takes us to Otto Vass, of course, 'cause you know, but for his mental illness he would be here.

LIZA stops the tape. Rewind. Stop. Play.

LAWYER 1:
Anyway, I'm surprised it happens as rarely as it does.

LIZA:
Uh, but—

LAWYER 1:
This takes us to Otto Vass, of course, 'cause you know, but for his mental illness he would be here.

LIZA stops the tape. Rewind. Stop. Play.

LAWYER 1:
Anyway, I'm surprised it happens as rarely as it does.

LIZA:
Uh, but—

LAWYER 1:
This takes us to Otto Vass, of course, 'cause you know, but for his mental illness he would be here.

The world begins to tilt. Is this really happening? The world slowly returns. LIZA fast-forwards the tape. The actors fast-forward, we hear the whirring sound, through a sequence involving plates cleared, legs crossed, uncrossed etc. LIZA eventually stops the tape.

SCENE 4

> *Later in the restaurant.*

LAWYER 1:

I used to tell a joke that I was going to give an embossed pencil out to the officers that said "Shut the Fuck Up" on it...

> *LAWYER 2 laughs.*

So as to prevent them from writing reports and their notes before they availed themselves of advice from either the association rep or a lawyer.

LAWYER 2:

Uh—

LAWYER 1:

The same advice, I might add, that lawyers give to their clients regularly when they deal with the authorities.

LAWYER 2:

Yeah, but there's a difference between cops and other people—

LAWYER 1:

I agree, except that—

LAWYER 2:

"I was in fear for my life—"

LAWYER 1:

Exactly. Or—

LAWYER 2:

You choose one of the following three phrases.

LAWYER 1:

Or, or to, to, um, to um, you know, reference the Use of Force Guideline—

> *As though conjured by LIZA's imagination, a large image of the Use of Force Continuum Wheel — a guideline used in policing to assess the amount of escalating force to use in a given situation — is projected above and behind LIZA and the LAWYERS.*

The image transforms into a kind of Dance Dance Revolution Wheel. The officers appear and perform dance movements that are also reminiscent of the physical altercation seen in Act I.

LIZA leaves the table and gets lost in between the dancing OFFICERS.

The dance stops. The scene resumes. Still feeling the reverberations of what has just occurred, LIZA returns to the table and refocuses on the luncheon.

LAWYER 2:
Yeah but—look, you're representing the subject officer and two witness officers, say—

LAWYER 1:
Uh huh.

LAWYER 2:
And you're—and you're very reasonable or you then talk to all those guys...

LAWYER 1:
Uh huh.

LAWYER 2:
—and say let's see, I wanna talk to these few guys... and I want you to be interviewed first but don't write anything yet 'cause you might convince... You know... and you manage that whole thing. I don't think it's reasonable at all.

LAWYER 1:
That's a fact of human nature that no division of labour among the lawyers is going to overcome. If the lawyer—if the police officers have already gotten together to decide what the story is gonna be—

LAWYER 2:
But they're supposed to be segregated—

LAWYER 1:
Oh, I know that, but—

LAWYER 2:
And, and, and they have one lawyer. It's ridiculous.

LIZA:
If officers aren't segregated…

LAWYER 1:
But generally they are.

LIZA:
But if—

LAWYER 2:
Yeah, but their lawyers aren't. That's the impression …

LAWYER 1:
…I don't think any SIU person would ever say that I ever jimmied the results of an investigation.

LAWYER 2:
No, no, no I wouldn't accuse you of doing that—

LAWYER 1:
No, I know, but that's how the conversation—

LAWYER 2:
Certainly not in a conscious way—

I mean subconsciously. I mean—

LAWYER 1:
Well, you know, if they want to alleviate the possible collateral effects of my active subconscious, I'm all in favour of it—

LAWYER 2:
Can I cross-examine you here?

LAWYER 1:
Yeah, sure.

LIZA fast-forwards the tape and we are now:

SCENE 5

In the courtroom.

All continue to sit in the restaurant, though they are now "in court."

OFFICER D:

We do get that training, especially with heavyset people, like, for example, if you were to arrest somebody who is obese and have them handcuffed to the back, which is how we handcuff, and put them into a police car laying down on their stomach and drive them to the station, chances are that the ten minutes that it takes to get there, the person might be dead when you get there.

LAWYER 2:

And you're acutely aware of this.

OFFICER D:

Yes.

LAWYER 2:

And for that reason he didn't spend more than five seconds on his tummy.

OFFICER D:

That's correct.

LAWYER 2:

And this is the first time that you've spoken publicly about any of this stuff.

OFFICER D:

That's right.

LAWYER 2:

You are aware that there was no blood found on your uniform or your boots, right?

OFFICER D:

I'm aware of that.

LAWYER 2:

And you didn't strike or kick Mr. Vass in any way.

OFFICER D:
No.

LAWYER 2:
Did you see Officer C kicking Mr. Vass?

OFFICER D:
No, I didn't.

OFFICER C:
I did not kick Mr. Vass. I was over his leg area. I may have brushed his leg.

LAWYER 2:
I put it to you that brushing would not have resulted in nine areas of contact stains.

OFFICER C:
Well, I did not kick Mr.Vass.

LAWYER 2:
You know, sir, the—the investigator was thinking that those stains were obtained by your making contact with something that had blood on it. And this was Mr. Vass's blood.

OFFICER C:
I'm a police officer, not a forensic scientist.

LAWYER 2:
Blood was found on Officers A and B, none was found on your partner Officer D. Can you give an explanation as to why, in the 33 seconds that you and your partner were there, you got so much of Mr. Vass's blood on you and your partner would have gotten none?

OFFICER C:
I don't know. As I explained, I was on the ground.

LAWYER 2:
Wasn't your partner on the ground some, sir?

OFFICER C:
I don't know. I didn't see him.

LAWYER 2:
You didn't see him at all?

OFFICER C:
No.

LAWYER 2:
You told the Crown attorney specifically that the lighting was good enough that you could read the fine print on the OHIP card outside, right?

OFFICER A:
Yes. That's right.

LAWYER 2:
Nonetheless, you didn't see any of the baton strikes that your partner did on Mr. Vass; is that right?

OFFICER A:
That's correct.

LAWYER 2:
And you didn't see any of the kicks that he gave to Mr. Vass, right?

OFFICER A:
No, I did not.

LAWYER 2:
And you didn't see any other officer in any way strike Mr. Vass; is that right? Throughout the entire event.

OFFICER A:
No. I was only concerned with what I was doing because of the volatile situation.

LAWYER 2:
You heard Constable B say that he didn't see anything that you did except for one palm strike around the gun?

OFFICER A:
He was, as I was, engrossed in what he was doing.

LAWYER 2:
This is what I said to you, sir: "He doesn't stop. He doesn't listen. He doesn't do what you told him, and by God, you're going to make him right?"

Answer: "No, That's not it. I was hoping Mr. Vass was—I can't make him do anything. He can keep resisting as long as he wants. He can resist until he dies. We can keep fighting."

Did you say that, sir?

OFFICER B:
Yes, I did.

LAWYER 2:
And he apparently did resist until he died, right?

OFFICER B:
No, when we had him in handcuffs he was no longer resisting. If Mr. Vass continues to struggle and continues to fight, and then he succumbs to whatever he succame to while I'm trying to take him into custody, unfortunately—I mean, that's the sad result here. But they are all Mr. Vass's choices, they are not mine.

LAWYER 2:
Mr. Vass chose to die that night, is your view, sir, is that right?

OFFICER B:
Mr. Vass chose to resist.

SCENE 6

Back in the restaurant.

WAITERS A and B holding down the service

LIZA:
Can I ask you... It's years later—where are the officers, and um, one of the things—that's my first question: Where are the officers?

LAWYER 1:
They're all on the job. Two of them have been promoted. A and D are both sergeants.

LIZA:
In which division?

LAWYER 1:

I think Officer D was up at 31 Division in the north end. I don't know where B went. He was in Hold Up...and he got promoted and I don't know where they put him.

LIZA:

What does that mean; he was "in hold up"?

LAWYER 1:

He was in the Hold Up Squad.

LIZA:

Oh, okay.

LAWYER 1:

He got promoted out of there and they signed him to a division and I don't think I even know. C is uh, is at 51 or 52, and he's working the street. And A is in Guns and Gangs. 'Cause he was at the shooting that I last did.

LIZA:

When you say "guns and gangs," what do you...

LAWYER 1:

It's a division of the police service. They go out and deal with guns and gangs.

LIZA:

Ha. Right.

LAWYER 1:

So that's what he's doing. And as far as I can tell, they're all doing fine.

LIZA:

One of things that I really want for the next steps of this project is, um, to speak to the officers. Do you think that any of them would speak to me?

Short pause.

LAWYER 1:

No.

LIZA:

Really? I think I might—I mean I could just phone up a division and ask them, but I was wondering if that might be something that you could… ask.

LAWYER 1:

You testified against them.

LIZA:

You know, I absolutely understand and respect the reasons for advising the officers not to speak with me but… (*Laughing.*)

LAWYER 1:

I do not plan on advising them not to speak to you. Officers are grown men who can make up their own minds. I think it unlikely in the extreme that they will want to discuss anything with you. But I do not speak for them.

> *All eat in extended silence. Sound of cutlery on plates heightens. Ambience heightens.*

> *LIZA finally asks the question on her mind.*

LIZA:

(*To LAWYER 1.*) Maybe…I know there was some discussion in this case, and maybe in others about the Blue Code of Silence. Can you speak to that? What's your take on it?

LAWYER 1:

Well, there isn't any evidence—they all testified.

LIZA:

In general—I'm just talking about—

LAWYER 1:

Well, (*Refers to LAWYER 2.*) ask him about that. He postulates that it exists, and I don't—

LAWYER 2:

(*Overlapping.*) It's not a question of not testifying; it's a question of what they say when they testify. (*Laughs.*) They testify the guy didn't do anything wrong when it's cops, no matter what the guy did.

LAWYER 1:

That's just—

LIZA:
I'm not talking about the specifics of this case, I'm talking generally...

LAWYER 2:
But just generally if someone just said—I think that everybody—nobody wants to be a tattletale, right? There have been a lot of specific studies demonstrating that this is pretty prevalent.

Pause.

LIZA:
You don't want to speak to that.

LAWYER 1:
Well, I mean, you know—

LAWYER 2:
(*Laughing.*) He has a code of silence. He's gonna be quiet.

LAWYER 1:
Yeah, exactly. I'm honouring the Blue Code of Silence.

The men eat.

SCENE 7

LAWYER 1:
So, what are you doing about Otto?

LIZA:
Um, well, I'm... just trying to, you know, get as much information... uh ...

LAWYER 1:
Oh. You missed my second *Annie Hall* joke. We called a psychiatrist up to testify about Otto's history of mental illness and the guy was, you know, as rigid and formal as you could ever imagine. I was the first up to cross-examine him. So I said, "Doc, have you ever seen that Woody Allen movie *Zelig*?" And His Honour went, (*Laughing.*) "Are you gonna do another Woody Allen thing?" Admittedly, inappropriate, because we're talking about people with mental illness and

dead people, but it was so grim at this point... It struck me
that we could all use a little bit of a break...

LIZA:

(*Agreeing.*) Sure.

> Beat.

LAWYER 1:

Excuse me.

> *LAWYER 1 gets up and heads out to speak on the phone.*
> *As he exits, he whispers to a WAITER that he will take*
> *the check.*

SCENE 8

> *Takes place immediately after the preceding scene.*

> *WAITERS clear the table during the following*
> *conversation.*

LIZA:

Any advice?

LAWYER 2:

It's gonna get harder. You have a very interesting story.
You know... there was a man named Kenneth Allen, who
was undergoing a cocaine psychosis and was frenzied, and
on the streetcar or something and just started screaming,
threatening people and so on. They called the police, the
police had to subdue him. There was no question, they
properly did that: they handcuffed him and brought him
back to 52 Division. But then something was discovered
by an OPP officer reviewing the case for the inquest...
You could see as he goes around the corner, his hands are
cuffed behind his back, the police officer has a night stick
across his throat and his head is poking through. If you
blink you'll miss it, and even if you don't blink you might
miss it. He's pulling him by his throat by the nightstick
through the police station.

LIZA:

Uh hmm.

LAWYER 2:

So, it was suggested that the neck bones of the deceased be examined again, and they showed cracks in the bones and so on... Yeah, really interesting in all sorts of ways. It became clear that this man was choked to death by the nightstick. The police officers got acquitted at trial—

LIZA:

Uh huh?

LAWYER 2:

—because the original pathologist said he died of cocaine poisoning.

LIZA:

Right.

LAWYER 2:

But at the inquest, the jury concluded that he died from the nightstick.

LIZA:

Right, but then you can't go back—

LAWYER 2:

And retry. No.

LIZA:

Huh. And what year was that?

LAWYER 2:

Must have been the '90s. Let me check the Google. I can find out more if you want to do a play about that.

> *LIZA laughs, and she exits off to go to the washroom, passing LAWYER 1 returning to the table.*

LAWYER 2:

I hope you're able to maintain your enthusiasm.

LAWYER 1:

Enthusiasm about what—

> *LIZA fast-forwards the tape.*

LIZA:

Um... I know um, we're winding down here with coffee. I wanted to ask—

LAWYER 1:

(*Referring to LAWYER 2.*) Ask him.

LIZA:

(*Laughing.*) I've asked him enough.

LAWYER 2:

(*Laughing.*) On behalf of my client, I—

> *LIZA isn't interested in this conversation. She fast-forwards the tape. When she stops, a WAITER who was pouring water suddenly becomes MICHAEL— Otto Vass's son. He begins to speak to LIZA. This is a surprise. What is this doing on this tape?*
>
> *The lawyers are frozen. Time has stopped for all but LIZA.*

SCENE 9

MICHAEL:

... He was a great dad. The average day: I'd come home from school, we'd hang out. Usually like, at 8 o'clock *The Simpsons* would come on. We'd watch that together...I still have some stuff that I keep close to me.

This one Pokemon card that I received from him... I still have that... It was one that was different from the rest. I remember going to the Ex here in Toronto. That was always fun. I remember he won this polar bear with a Coca-Cola bottle. That was really awesome. He'd always be there. I remember friends' dads, either they were too strict or not strict at all. He was like a hybrid of both.

When I heard my dad was mentally ill, it was actually a few weeks after he died. When I came back from Hungary, I learned that he died, like, a day after. A few weeks after, Mom told me he was mentally ill. I was shocked because personally I had never seen him mentally ill. So, it was really interesting when I heard he had such a problem because I never experienced it. I could say that he's more normal than other parents I would meet. It's quite interesting. (*Awkward laugh.*) Ha ha....

...I guess I'm quite similar to him. Ha ha.

LIZA:
How so?

MICHAEL:
I guess someone would say looks, but also the way I look at life—like in a fun way, differently. I was eight years old when he died so I can't really... I try and—

The courtroom interrupts.

SCENE 10
In the courtroom.

An image of court transcripts flashes onto the floor.

LAWYER 2:
Now, sir, there's something called a code of silence or a "Blue Code of Silence" among officers. Police officers develop, for obvious reasons, a kind of camaraderie when they work together.

OFFICER A:
Of course. It's a job. Like any other, I guess.

LAWYER 2:
Sometimes there are tense situations when police officers work together and they are called upon to use force against other human beings, right?

OFFICER A:
If you have to, yes.

LAWYER 2:
And there's at least the potential that some officers might use excessive force in some situations, right?

OFFICER A:
In some situations, but not this situation.

LAWYER 2:
I'm talking more generally now.

OFFICER A:
I can't comment on hypotheticals. But to agree with your hypothetical, maybe, yeah.

LAWYER 2:
There are a couple of lawyer jokes that come to mind but I'm going to refrain. Sir, have you heard any case where a police officer reported another police officer for using excessive force?

OFFICER A:
I can't say if I have or haven't.

LAWYER 2:
Well, you can say you have or haven't, sir. Have you—

OFFICER A:
I've heard—again, this is speculation and rumours. But I have heard over the years that other police officers might have. I heard of one situation where they didn't understand why the person had to use force. Years ago.

LAWYER 2:
Are you saying that an officer reported another officer for that, sir?

OFFICER A:
I don't say "reported," but he was concerned why force was used.

LAWYER 2:
Like for example if you had seen your partner hitting Mr. Vass on the legs as he described in court and you had thought that was excessive, you might have to say to him, quietly, "Hey, maybe next time you don't have to keep on hitting him that much. You could back off a little bit, right?"

OFFICER A:
If that scenario took place, in a perfect world, I would have stopped him. But I didn't see him do any of that.

LAWYER 2:
Right. You didn't see him hitting at all?

OFFICER A:
So I can't comment on that.

LAWYER 2:
But I'm suggesting that you would never, ever, ever, report to any authorities that he had to use excessive force, in your view. That's what you would never do and that's what the code of silence precludes.

OFFICER A:
I disagree with you, sir.

LAWYER 2:
You disagree.

OFFICER A:
I joined this job—I have a lot of integrity. I joined this job to help people… Am I saying that it never happens? No. No. But I've never in the ten years of my being a police officer had occasions to have that come across. The "Blue Code of Silence" or what do you call it? The blue, or code of silence, wouldn't affect me. It's not something that police officers talk about if there is a code of silence…They are just normal everyday people that have families like everyone else and you just do your job.

SCENE 11

The world shifts back to the restaurant and to the end of the luncheon.

The LAWYERS and LIZA are getting up from the table.

LAWYER 1:
Anyway… I'll tell you what shows I saw—what I liked. My last two trips to Broadway I went to see *Promises, Promises.*

LAWYER 2:
Ahh, yeah.

LAWYER 1:

And *Chicago*—Miss Chenoweth was pretty winsome. But before that I saw *A Little Night Music* with Stritch and Bernadette Peters, which was great.

> *As LAWYER 1 pays the tab, the OFFICERS enter in full uniform. The LAWYERS and LIZA notice them.*

LAWYER 1:

In Stratford I saw *The Tempest* with uh, Plummer. I didn't like it. I saw, uh, *The Winter's Tale*, which was superb. Uh, what else did I see? I saw the musical *Peter Pan* which was superb. I couldn't believe how good it was.

LIZA:

Uh—

LAWYER 1:

Well I thought that McCann, uh McCann, is that his name? You know he played the narrator and Hook—

LIZA:

Tom McCamus.

LAWYER 1:

I mean he was great. I thought it worked. I thought the set was superb. The music was good, I thought the whole thing was well done.

> *The LAWYERS begin to exit.*

LAWYER 2:

Hey, I hope I'm played by a very good-looking guy.

LAWYER 1:

I also saw *Les Liaisons Dangereuses*, which was terrific. I couldn't believe it was one-third empty. That was superb. So I had a pretty good run at Stratford. The only thing I missed was *As You Like It*, which I heard was only good and not great. So I didn't feel too bad. I like to see everything that they do, but ya gotta give up something...

SCENE 12

LIZA watches the LAWYERS leave. During the following, recorded voices are heard.

The OFFICERS head to the ARTIST's drawing on the ground of Otto Vass. They pick up the portrait and carry it upstage as though they are pallbearers. A kind of funeral procession begins, as the actors lift the image of Otto Vass and carry it upstage toward the back of the playing area. During this, the names of those who died at the hands of the police over the past several years are projected onto the floor and the walls, creating a kind of silent scroll throughout the space. Names might include: Sammy Yatim, Sylvia Klibingaitis, Edmund Yu, Andrew Loku, Reyal Jardine-Douglas, Byron Debassige, Robert Dziekanski, Charles McGillivary, Kenneth Allen, Douglas Minty, Levi Schaeffer, Michael Eligon... (The list of names should reflect the year and place in which the show is produced.)

The list continues to grow and overwhelms the space; a litany of names honouring the dead.

The scene becomes a cacophony of sound, voice, image and memory.

LIZA crosses down to the ARTIST as this happens.

We hear:

VOICE 1:
In '85 Vass pleaded guilty to setting fire to a rental property he owned while the tenants were still in the house.

VOICE 2:
"He takes some medication and when he doesn't take it he goes really mental."

VOICE 3:
"He was very kind. He would go out of his way to help somebody. He would not hurt anybody."

VOICE 4:
"He was just emotionally unstable."

VOICE 5:
Vass's friend, a local landlord, said Vass was harmless. "I never saw him as a violent man."

VOICE 6:
"He hung around a lot of people who were doing illegal stuff, I guess."

VOICE 7:
He had been under some stress after the death of his mother, a co-worker said.

VOICE 8:
In the weeks preceding his death, Mrs. Vass tried her damnedest to get her troubled husband help.

VOICE 9:
A friend said that he had wanted to organize a local committee to improve the neighbourhood.

VOICE 10:
"He was always trying to better himself."

VOICE 11:
"Another eyewitness—

LIZA possibly acknowledges herself at this moment.

—who didn't give her name but was also interviewed by the SIU, said she was too exhausted to talk."

VOICE OF THE CORONER:
His "sudden unexpected cardiac death" at 1:45 AM was due to: "Acute anxiety and excited delirium in a man with long-standing bipolar disorder, in association with cardiovascular stress resulting from violent struggle and morbid obesity." Cause of death…Undetermined.

SCREEN:
INTERMISSION

END OF ACT II

Syrus Marcus Ware and Sarah Kitz. Photo by Kyle Purcell.

Officers cross-examination. With David Ferry, Brett Donahue, RH Thomson and company. Photo by Kyle Purcell.

PART TWO

Bruised Years Choir. Photo by Kyle Purcell.

Dance party. Photo by Aislinn Rose.

Act III

NOTES ON PART TWO

The material that follows reflects the ways in which the production at the Luminato Festival presented each segment. (You will note the inclusion of the names of this production's company members.) While Part Two has a clear foundation and form and includes sections of verbatim text from the *Out the Window* archives, it is a malleable entity inspired and envisioned by director Sarah Garton Stanley and created though collaboration with the company.

TIMING:

Part Two lives in the present. We are in a theatre in real time. As such, each performance will be different; each is a variation on a theme, the theme being: Community. The theatre space itself becomes the container for Community, one that is ultimately shared equally by both the audience and performers alike.

There is a running order and strict timing throughout this 45-minute act. In fact, timing these segments forms a structure that allows for greater freedom in the piece as a whole. As noted in the dialogue, these timings are connected to the death of Otto Vass:

45 Minutes: The approximate amount of time that Vass received CPR before the ambulance arrived.

6 Minutes: The approximate time between Vass leaving the store and his death.

3 Minutes: The approximate time between the first punch and Vass's death.

33 Seconds: The approximate time between the arrival of the second set of officers and Vass's death.

These times are also projected on the screen as they are being described by the actor introducing the particular segment.

THE STAGE:

In Toronto, the company invited the audience to join them on stage at various points in the act. This was an easy, open invitation, not an expectation. Several dozens of audience members took us up on this invitation at each performance. They were invited to come and go as they pleased, to share in the meal being provided, to get a closer look at Syrus Ware's Gallery of Lost Lives, and to participate if they wanted, or simply to choose to sit or stand and watch. It is essential that the company make sure that anyone who joins them on stage feels welcomed, well taken care of through the act, and acknowledged.

GUESTS:

We invited a guest to speak for six minutes at each performance. This was intended to offer and ignite various perspectives and voices about the project's themes and issues: Policing, madness, justice, racism—and where we find ourselves within these themes in the present.

These guests included activists, political leaders, social workers, members of Black Lives Matter, the Empowerment Council (which is involved in policing and mental illness), and even a highly articulate ten-year-old girl—a daughter of one of the actors in the show.

THE LONG TABLE:

Ultimately, Part Two becomes a "long table conversation." It is created by the artists involved and reflects the community in which it is being produced. There can and should be disagreement, argument, support, humour, play and, one hopes, excellent listening, care and respect. And snacks.

Timing is strict throughout this act. When the DING sounds, the speaker stops speaking, regardless of where they are in their story.

1. BRUISED YEARS CHOIR

(Song 1: "Trouble in Mind" by Richard M. Jones.)
The choir is onstage for places.
LX: Lose house light on choir.
PROJECTION: Add title: "The Bruised Years Choir"
VIDEO: The 45-minute clock starts as they begin to sing.
End of song.
SFX: DING.

2. MONOLOGUE

3 MINUTES

The actor playing LIZA (Sarah) enters from the choir and sits onstage. The following monologue offers a passageway for the audience into the world of Part Two.

So. That's what happened.
Or—That's a version of what happened.
I mean, there's enough material for another three acts.

Liza Balkan got to know his wife. And she also met some mental health experts, some activists, some neighbours...a police psychologist... the judge... Liza interviewed several cops. Not THE cops. Well... She did call one of them after she learned which division he was at. She said he was very polite, she was very polite; everyone was very polite. She asked if she might interview him some day. He was probably as shocked as shit by that phone call as she was. I can appreciate why he never called her back.
This was Officer...D.
No names. Liza is still nervous about being sued. She also expressed concern for the fact that the officers have families and kids and it is many years ago...
(Room here to comment about this if you choose.)
Of course, you can check the Google.

There are boxes and boxes of versions of what happened.
Still…
(*Beat.*)
The perspective from out that window, is only… It's half a block.
In a city—in a country—filled with blocks.
So…
This turns out not to have been a show about the details of what happened in the 7-Eleven prior to the altercation in the parking lot.
Or the other witness accounts.
Or the multiple injuries Mr. Vass sustained that night.
Or about the officers being found not guilty of all charges.
Or about the complexities of the case.
Or how the term "excited delirium" is a diagnosis only ever used in relation to incidents involving the police.
This is not the show with a scene where Liza divulges the cost of all those court transcripts. Pages and pages filled with Lawyers 1 and 2. And others. And Officers ABCD. And others.
Liza was advised by lawyers not to use any real names.
Except her own. And the victim. Mr. Vass. The man she met from her window during those few minutes between his leaving the 7-Eleven and his death.
This turns out not to really be about any of that.
This is about …
A blank space.
My name is Sarah
There will be snacks.

SFX: DING.

3. CHOIR

(Gnarls Barkley's "Crazy.")
End of song.
LX: Dim as Choir exits.

4. LAND ACKNOWLEDGEMENT

33 SECONDS

The actor playing LIZA (Sarah) begins giving a land acknowledgement. She is most likely interrupted by—

SFX: DING.

ACTOR 1 (Richard): TIME!

SFX: Brahms' "Hungarian Dance #5."

5. TABLES

33 SECONDS

Company enters with 3 long tables. During the following, one long vertical table is created CS.
Actors come to DSR LX to deliver their information.

ACTOR 2 (Brett): We are telling this part of the story in increments of time.

VIDEO: 33 seconds clock.

ACTOR 4 (James): 33 seconds. (The time my character and Richard's character were on the scene before Otto Vass died.)

VIDEO: 3-minute clock.

ACTOR 5 (David): 3 minutes. (The time of the altercation between Brett's character and Peyson's character, including the arrival of James's and Richard's characters' arrival.)

VIDEO: 6-minute clock.

ACTOR 6 (Robert): 6 minutes. The time it reportedly took from the time Vass exited the store to—

SFX: DING.
SFX: Music cuts out.

ACTOR 1 (Richard): STOP. I am the timekeeper; nobody else wanted the job. 33 seconds is up.

6. THE ARTIST

3 MINUTES

The ARTIST talks about reasons for doing this show/this work.

ARTIST (Syrus): My name is Syrus Marcus Ware... Oh. Wait. Get the food...
The company gets food, bowls of snacks, plates, cutlery, etc. during the rest of the monologue.

ARTIST: I am part of Black Lives Matter Toronto...

ARTIST continues to speak: This is how I identify/ who I am; this is why I am here. For example: Identifies as black, transgendered, dealing with mental illness...

SFX: DING.

7. HONOURING OTTO VASS AND HIS SEAT AT THE TABLE

33 SECONDS

ACTOR 4 (James): My name is James, I played Officer D. We decided on a meal, a way to honour Otto Vass. He was Hungarian so…we planned for Hungarian Goulash. It is something we all could share. Real Liza heard from his wife that he also loved pizza. But you know: Carbs. And he loved Queen. Join us, at any point. (It's vegetarian.)

SFX: Song: "We Are the Champions" by Queen.
SFX: DING.

ACTOR 1 (Richard) adds a "STOP." (Or whatever.)

8. AUDIENCE MEMBER BECOMES A COP

3 MINUTES

ACTOR 1 (Richard): I am the fight director on the show and we did a lot of work training in basic police practices. Is there a volunteer from the audience who would like to volunteer?
We might take a picture or two. Are you okay with this? (Etc.)

VIDEO PREP #1: for taking photo of audience member. (To go back screen.)
VIDEO PREP #2: for taking photo of audience member on table. (To go back screen.)
SFX: DING.

ACTOR 1 (Richard) thanks volunteer and offers them a seat at the table.

9. THAT CORNER

33 SECONDS

ACTOR 3 (Peyson): Wild! I live right by that corner. Cops slowed down the other day as I was walking by. It was nothing. But it made me feel/think what if it had been a something...

SFX: DING.

ACTOR 1 or OTHERS add a "STOP." (Or whatever.)

10. THE GALLERY

3 MINUTES

The ARTIST (Syrus) brings the focus to the Gallery—the drawings he had done of those who have lost their lives. He focuses on a particular portrait at each performance, offering information about the life of the person who died. For example:

ARTIST: This is Andrew Loku... I want to tell you a little bit about him. He died in 12 seconds...

ARTIST (Syrus) invites audience members to come onto the stage to look at the Gallery. They are welcome to stay as long as they like. Or to leave at any time. The COMPANY will offer them seats at the table, food, etc.

SFX: DING.

11. INTRODUCING THE GUEST SPEAKER

3 MINUTES

The actor who played LAWYER 2 (RH Thomson) talks about family at the table in the room and introduces the guest speaker. He asks audience members to: "Join us, down here, at any point."

SFX: DING.
VIDEO: 6-minute clock.
PROJECTION: (Name of guest speaker.)

12. GUEST SPEAKER

6 MINUTES

SFX: DING.

13. WHAT DO YOU THINK?

3 MINUTES

The ARTIST and ACTORS ask the audience what they think thus far. They will choose a volunteer from the audience to share their thoughts.

SFX: DING.

ACTOR 1 thanks volunteer and offers them a seat at the table.

14. INTERACTIONS WITH COPS

33 SECONDS

The actor who played LAWYER 1 (David Ferry) asks about actors' and audience members' interactions with cops...

SFX: DING.

ACTOR 1 (Richard) thanks a volunteer and offers them a seat at the table.

15. OFFICERS ON THE STAND

6 MINUTES

Projections of transcripts are flashed on to the floor.

OFFICERS A and B are on the witness stand.

OFFICER A: I don't agree with that, sir.

LAWYER 2: You don't agree with that.

OFFICER A: I don't agree with your terminology that he was beaten, because he wasn't beaten.

LAWYER 2: Hitting him until he dies, sir.

OFFICER A: That's fine. If you—how would you know—first of all, what we did didn't cause his death. That was already determined at the trial.

Transcripts continue to be projected on to the stage and playing area as the scene continues.

OFFICER B: I'm sitting here in an inquest trying to help the jury determine how Mr. Vass died.

LAWYER 2: Are you?

OFFICER B: And help find recommendations to prevent this from happening again.

LAWYER 2: I see. And do you think that your beating of him might have contributed to that death, sir?

OFFICER B: I did not beat him, sir.

LAWYER 2: I'm not an expert but do you recall in court when I suggested an alternate scenario? That is, you backing off and pepper spraying. Do you recall that?

OFFICER B: Yes.

LAWYER 2: He's a man in his fifties. He's a fat, out-of-shape guy. He's on his back on the ground. You both back up to have the optimal three-to-six feet and then you spray him. Wouldn't that have been a better scenario in retrospect, sir?

OFFICER B: The fact that he would be alive today would be a great scenario. Unfortunately, the scenario for using pepper spray never presented itself to us.

LAWYER 2: You could have made it present yourself, sir. He's lying on the ground. You're near him. You back up. You yell: "Partner, back up, pepper spray!" And you both back up to opposite sides and you spray him.

OFFICER B: I don't believe that scenario presented itself. I wish it could have but it didn't.

LAWYER 2: Sir, I'm suggesting that you had to create the scenario. "Partner, back up. Pepper spray."

OFFICER B: If we were to somehow say, Mr. Vass, you stay there, and we're just going to get away and stand back and spray you with pepper spray. That scenario is unreasonable.

LAWYER 2: In what way is it unreasonable, sir?

OFFICER B: At the risk of repeating myself over and over again.

LAWYER 2: You are, sir, but you're not telling me the problem with it.

LAWYER 1: Excuse me, how many times are we going to go through this? I mean, my friend thinks that cross-examination is the equivalent of rock breaking.

LAWYER 2: Okay. Let me try to set the stage better.

OFFICER A: Sure.

LAWYER 2: There's a man on the ground. He's been hit with a baton for a while. He's gotten a few relatively soft and one really good palm in the jaw. Would you agree that if you thought, gee, the man is not stopping, this is getting dangerous here for him, would you agree that the risk, whatever you judge it as, the possible risk of him getting up and hurting you before you could push him down again, before you could pepper spray him, before you could hit him with a baton, before you could do anything, is small enough that it would be worth taking that risk rather than continuing to hit him until he died?

OFFICER A: Well, to finally answer your question in a way that hopefully I can express, is that I wouldn't change a thing.

LAWYER 2: So you're very consistent with what your partner said, "He can resist until he dies," right?

OFFICER A: I didn't say that.

LAWYER 2: Your partner also said at trial, and I put it to him here: "Mr. Vass was the author of what happened that night. Mr. Vass attacked me. Mr. Vass continued to attack me." Do you agree that Mr. Vass was the author of what happened that night, sir?

OFFICER A: Unfortunately, how it might be, I do.

LAWYER 2: And you don't think that even in retrospect—

OFFICER A: I would have reacted the same way.

LAWYER 2: The same way, okay.

OFFICER A: Again, I'm repeating myself over and over and over again. I truly believe that what I did was right. I have, more than most, 99 percent of the people on this job, an empathy towards people who suffer from mental illness. I cared for these people. I still care for these people. I feel, and it's unfortunate, that I think society in general let this person down, not the police. We're being blamed, unfortunately. We're the last line of defence. We're supposed to be a social worker. We're supposed to be a psychologist. Even with my extra training, that night only dealt with a use of force issue. I wish I would have known his past. I wish I would have known Mr. Vass before that night. I wish there was some way that his violence or medical history was on the computer. I think the whole system let him down.

Unfortunately, I, as a police officer that night, had to come across Mr. Vass. Unfortunately, I can't go back in time and force Mr. Vass to be on his meds. There's a lot of "What ifs." If I would have known that he was mentally ill, I would have called for more back up. There's a lot of things—

LAWYER 2: I'm sorry, sir, I didn't hear you.

OFFICER A: If I would have known that he was mentally ill and he had tried to kill people in the past, he tried to burn people in the past, he went for an officer's gun in the past, if I would have known how he could be Mr. Nice Guy one minute and snap and be one of the most violent schizophrenics that has ever been—that I've encountered—obviously he needed help. It's not his problem that he suffered from this mental disease. He's a victim of his own disease. There's a lot of "What ifs" I would have changed. But I still believe that I would have done the same thing. I only have a problem with your scenario because you're assuming that what we did, what I did, caused his death. It's a scenario that I don't want to go down that road because I don't believe in that. I truly believe that what we did was authorized. We had to deal with it the best way we could.

There is silence until the full six minutes are up, approximately 5–7 seconds.

SFX: DING.

16. DANCE PARTY

3 MINUTES

A dance party for all who care to dance.
Folded sections of tin foil are passed around on deck during the dance. The ARTIST will later show guests how to use them.

SFX: DING.

17. OUR METHODS

33 SECONDS

ACTOR 2 (Brett) speaks to how this is old territory. How we know that our methods do not work.

SFX: DING.
PROJECTION: "Verbatim interview between Liza Balkan and a theatre director who lived in the same building and worked at a shelter called Street City."

18. INTERVIEW WITH A NEIGHBOUR

3 MINUTES

TWO ACTORS (Richard and Sarah.) Sarah explains that several officers entered the director's apartment en masse to see if his view included the parking lot. When it was clear that his window faced elsewhere, they all left. Without a word. The ACTORS read this transcript together.

LIZA: Can you tell me a little about your work at Street City?

DIRECTOR: Where I worked, we had a woman Victoria, who, uh, was from the islands, a Caribbean woman, and she truly believed that there were evil spirits living under her bed. And so she would spray water under her bed and she would bang. Spray, spray, spray, bang and bang and bang. And you can imagine that. After six hours of this, the other tenants are ready to, you know, murder her. They're just going out of their minds and she's screaming. A cop shows up from 52 Division— somebody had called the police on her—and he walks up to the lady and he says, "Excuse me, ma'am. I'm going to take care of this for you. I want you to move. Would you kindly leave me alone in the room 'cause I need to shut the door." And he shuts the door. This guy was very clever. So he starts banging. "YOU GET OUTTA HERE, YOU!" BANG BANG BANG! "DON'T EVER COME BACK!" BANG BANG BANG BANG BANG BANG! Banging on the floor. "I'M TELLING YOU, DON'T YOU EVER COME BACK!" BANG BANG BANG BANG! He opens the door and he says, "If they ever come back, I want you to hold on to this or put it on." And he handed her the little tin foil Viking helmet that he had just made. And the smile on this woman's face…you've never seen anything like it in your life. And she just totally calmed down, because somebody had heard her. Somebody did not deny her reality… you know? Somebody really tried to attempt to take care of her problem and didn't say: "You crazy lady, there's nobody under your bed." So you really have to go to them. You really have to go to their reality and understand where they're at because they're not coming to you.

LIZA: Anything else?

DIRECTOR: What I think ultimately cost Otto Vass's life is that, you know, he had guys that thought he was, you know, an aggressive and violent man, when in actual fact they were dealing with a very severe mental health issue. The way I think they responded to it was, was you know, very emotional. And we don't deal with emotion very well in society. We try to beat it down—quite literally.

A demonstration: The ARTIST offers a lesson on how to make a tin foil hat.

19. A PATHWAY

33 SECONDS

Sarah, the actor playing LIZA, explains how we all wanted to do something that could offer a channel, a pathway, and option to feeling better.

20. I REMEMBER

6 MINUTES

VIDEO: A video of the real Liza Balkan.

The real Liza says: I remember him standing I remember him sitting with his legs out in front of him I remember him lying on his side in foetal position being kicked—okay, in the, in the stomach? But being kicked.
I remember a baton flying through the air—an officer running to it. I remember two more officers running in. I remember yelling "STOP." I remember turning off my lights, so I wouldn't be seen. I remember calling my boyfriend three times, leaving blow-by-blows on his voicemail.
I remember jumping back. I remember saying, "No, get back there and watch." Okay, I live alone—
I talk to myself.
... I remember my boyfriend finally calling me back. He had erased the messages.
I remember having binoculars in my hand. Seeing closer.
I remember talking to Vass's widow, Zsuzsanna, and her telling me all about the trip to Hungary they went on just a few short weeks before the incident. How they went dancing... *(Pause.)* But that wasn't August 9th, that conversation was...?
Days, weeks, months ago...whatever. You know, time....

Back to the night:

I remember asking my boyfriend if I should go downstairs and talk to the detective that was now on the scene. I remember his saying: "No."

I DON'T remember walking down the five flights. I remember approaching the detective. I remember the light shining inside the truck, or the car?... I just remember the brightness of this light against the darkness of the sky and the artificial lighting of the parking lot. The shadow of this detective's face. From 14th Division. The *same* division.

I didn't give my name or my address.

I remember a guy on a bike, on my right—stage right.

I DON'T remember walking back up the five flights.

I DON'T remember falling asleep.

I DO remember seeing the white truck down below. The SIU insignia. I remember introducing myself.

I seem to remember a beating.

I *remember* a beating.

The real Liza Balkan is at a paper shredder. Bankers Boxes surround. Liza begins to shred documents: Script/ transcript, the stuff of "versions." The sound of shredding leads to the intro of the song.

21. EVERYBODY HURTS

PART OF THE 6 MINUTES

The Bruised Years Choir sings "Everybody Hurts" by REM.
VIDEO: The lyrics of "Everybody Hurts" are projected on the screen.
End of song.

CURTAIN CALL

The curtain call involves everyone who is presently on the stage: actors, choir and audience members who have joined.
Everybody onstage bows.

MUSIC: "We Are the Champions" by Queen.
END OF SHOW

Post-show conversation with Tanisha Taitt, Liza Balkan, Sarah Kitz, Syrus Marcus Ware, Sarah Garton Stanley, Rosina Kazi. Photo by Aislinn Rose.

SUPPLEMENTAL MATERIALS

Timeline of the Event

August 9, 2000: Mr. Otto Vass died during an altercation with the police in a parking lot by a 7-Eleven at College and Lansdowne Streets in the west end of Toronto. Four officers were charged with manslaughter: Constables Philip Duncan, Robert LeMaitre, Filippo Bevilacqua, and Nam Le. All were acquitted. Mr. Vass was 55 years old, of Hungarian descent, and a husband and a father. He also had a history of mental illness.

2002: Preliminary hearing.

2003: Trial. Officers found not guilty in the death of Mr. Vass.

2006: Inquest. It concluded that his "sudden unexpected cardiac death at 1:45 AM was due to: acute anxiety and excited delirium in a man with long-standing bipolar disorder, in association with cardiovascular stress resulting from violent struggle and morbid obesity. Cause of death, undetermined."

The corner of College and Lansdowne, taken in 2008. The loft apartment above it where I lived: top floor, second full set of windows from the right. Photo by Trevor Schwellnus.

A Brief History of *Out the Window*
Liza Balkan, with contributions from artists involved in the play's development
Lab Cab Installation

This first iteration was a response to my experience of the journey through the justice system as a result of coming forward as a witness to the death of Mr. Vass in the summer of 2000. Lab Cab curator Aviva Armour-Ostroff invited me to participate in the festival. I grabbed this as an opportunity to share the literal and figurative overload of material that swirled around my internal and external living space: the still visceral memory of the violence that night, alongside hundreds of pages of court transcript from my time on the witness stand at the preliminary hearing in 2002, the trial in 2003 and the coroner's inquest in 2006. The installation was an attempt to make sense of what I felt at the time was impossible senselessness. I created a room filled with hundreds of pages of transcripts as well as action figures and audio recordings made from transcribed court proceedings. Was it just a form of art

Liza at Lab Cab Installation, 2007. Photo by Stephen Sparks.

therapy? Possibly. Was I looking for closure? Probably. All I knew was it was something I had to do, and I was given the space in which to do it. I figured that would be the end of it. It wasn't.

The following was recorded by some colleagues and included in the 10-minute performance portion of the installation. It is among the verbatim material that continues to live in the piece. Indeed, my reaction to experiencing this kind of cross-examination on the stand in a trial for manslaughter is among the many reasons I felt compelled to create the installation. That, and the greater disconnect between what I witnessed—what I still believed I witnessed—that night, my experience on the stand, and the outcome of the trial and inquest.

LAWYER 1:
  Ms. Balkan, I have a few questions, if I may.

LIZA:
  Yes.

LAWYER 1:
  I prefer to ask my questions from stage left, to use your term.

LIZA:
  That would be stage right from my perspective.

LAWYER 1:
  From your perspective.

LIZA:
  From my perspective.

LAWYER 1:
  Ma'am, had you ever seen anything like this before?

LIZA:
  No. Not in—not in real life. No.

LAWYER 1:
  In the movies you mean?

LIZA:
  Movies, TV. Whatever.

LAWYER 1:
  TV! So... it must have shocked you.

LIZA:
Yes, indeed.

LAWYER 1:
Now the beginning—well, you're in the acting business, right?

LIZA:
Yes, I am.

LAWYER 1:
And directing?

LIZA:
Yes.

LAWYER 1:
All right. Uh. Oh, are we talking about theatre, movies, or TV?

LIZA:
Primarily theatre.

LAWYER 1:
(*Clearly disappointed.*) Oh. Okay. So you know then, as someone who directs others, if not acts in these things, that the beginning of these things is important, right?

LIZA:
Yes.

LAWYER 1:
Because it often explains why people do what they do?

LIZA:
Uh hmm.

LAWYER 1:
Is that right?

LIZA:
Yes...

LAWYER 1:
And if you're working with a bunch of actors about doing a scene, the motive for the characters in the scene is crucial to how you act in it, right?

LIZA:

Yes.

LAWYER 1:

In fact, that probably forms a large part of the discussion between the director and the actors, right?

LIZA:

Yes.

LAWYER 1:

Everybody gets together, and having read the script or the play or whatever, and says why are Dorothy and John behaving the way they are, right?

LIZA:

That would be correct. Have you acted?

LAWYER 1:

No. But I've seen a few act—actors, I mean.

The stuff of Residency. Research. Recordings. Transcripts. Boxes. Photo by Liza Balkan.

Residency at The Theatre Centre

In 2008 The Theatre Centre invited me to develop the piece through its Residency Program and I am forever grateful. It was the start of the village that has brought this piece forward, and where it began its journey as the most malleable of projects: morphing in size, scope, and perspective each time.

Franco Boni

Former General and Artistic Director of The Theatre Centre:

Out the Window joined The Theatre Centre Residency Program in 2008. It remains one of the most remarkable and transformative theatrical processes I have ever experienced. On day one of Residency, Liza showed up with a handful of Bankers Boxes stuffed with court transcripts and research material. She was convinced that the truth about what happened to Otto Vass, and the story she wanted to tell about the truth, lay somewhere inside those boxes. With every development period the Bankers Boxes would multiply. By year four of Residency, Liza was surrounded. Boxes and boxes stuffed with court documents, transcripts and interviews.

After an emotional and successful run at the Free Fall Festival, *Out the Window* went dormant and the boxes were packed for storage. Six years to make the work, and another six to get it back to the stage.

To prepare for the Luminato production, Liza pulled out the boxes. Some were missing. There were a few weeks of panic, but the truth was that the story no longer lived inside those boxes. Liza knew it. Her revolution and the brilliance of Sarah Garton Stanley's direction made it clear that *Out the Window* was now not about an individual bearing witness, but about collective action.

During the first year of Residency, I invited designers Trevor Schwellnus, Michelle Ramsay and Thomas Ryder Payne into the process. We investigated the material aurally, visually and physically. Soundscape and scenography emerged. Actors recorded pages and pages of transcript. Thomas composed haunting music to accompany certain passages of dialogue. Trevor created footage from the College and Lansdowne location, shooting from multiple vantage points, including the one from my window and an imagined walk in Mr. Vass's footsteps from his shop down the street to the parking lot where he died.

The Theatre Centre was then housed in the Great Hall building at 1087 Queen Street West, just a few doors down from where it is now located. We worked in the basement and its upstairs wrap-around gallery. A good portion of what was created during these sessions found their way into the project's various presentations between 2009 and 2012. A particular and favourite creation ultimately never found a home in the piece: I remember Naomi Campbell joining our session on this day. It involved her dropping single transcript pages from the balcony of the rehearsal hall some thirty or forty feet in the air. When they

Fallen transcripts creating a broken image of a broken corner of the city. Photo by Trevor Schwellnus.

landed, a broken vision of the apartment building and corner where the incident occurred slowly emerged. Trevor projected the shot on to the dark floor. It was invisible until it came to fractured life, piece by piece, as each page landed. Oh, the vibrant discoveries that lie dormant on ye ole' cardboard cutting room floor of a Bankers Box.

Trevor Schwellnus

Set Designer / Scenographer:

From the beginning, *Out the Window* felt very personal. It was somebody's experience of being abused by a system that was meant to protect its citizens. When you are white and you have privilege, you walk through the world without knowing how good you have it. You're aware that people have issues and problems that are different than yours. And the scale of those is something that you can acknowledge, but not really, totally understand. But then, every once in a while, the system comes along and hits you in the head when you're trying to do the right thing. And you suddenly see the scale of a fucking huge social problem. This is one of those stories.

It's a story about seeing these problems as systemic, and not unusual bugs in our policy-making: Problems of racism, of systems that create impunity, and of the exposure of newcomers to Canada, of racialized communities, and of people with cognitive challenges, of the shortcomings in our collective management of our safety.

When Liza Balkan asked me to help her build environments in which she could tell this story, we started with a confessional approach with open space populated with papers. Reports, testimonies, court documents—we recreated her lived experience as a witness to a killing, a story that centred her in conflict with a legal system, and that drew upon the voices of the police officers involved. We scrutinized policies around "use-of-force" guidelines and police training.

In fairly short order we found that this was an issue that many more voices needed to participate in: At our table we sat a host of protagonists to read and consider the case surrounding the death of Otto Vass. We played with how the audience sees things: from opposing banks, like a parliament in judgment, to a simple front-on view, to being invited to read at the table.

And as the project grew and took on its final iteration, newly-energized movements affected our dramaturgies: Our table became a place to convene prominent leaders fighting for justice for Black and Indigenous victims of police violence, local politicians, citizens who have lost loved ones. Our stage—which had begun with paper and a microphone—welcomed projection, fight choreography, and 3D virtual environments. And our voices—which were launched by the resolve of one woman—became a chorus.

The 25-minute Rhubarb showing provided an opportunity to incorporate some of what was uncovered and developed during our early Residency. The piece was intriguing and, apparently, compelling. It added one other actor emerging from the audience as the voice of the lawyer for the defence. But the piece had no arc beyond a woman—me—attempting to sort through the remnants of a violent incident and its aftermath.

Chris Abraham / Crow's Theatre

Under Crow's Theatre Artistic Director Chris Abraham's guidance and direction, the scope and form of *Out the Window*'s storytelling expanded exponentially. Chris had heard me speak about the project at an event and expressed interest in working on it with me. Chris's directorial work was and is provocative, challenging, complex and thrilling. It was an exhilarating offer. I said yes. How could I not?

It was during this Crow's Residency that the project evolved into a deeper investigation of issues surrounding police culture, use of force, police violence and the justice system. We began to acquire the court testimony of the officers—and others—involved. The project was no longer just about my own time on the stand—the viewpoint of a single witness—but rather, we began to hear other voices and perspectives involved in the case itself, and in the subject matter in general. My testimony was still involved in the process, as was my own presence on stage. A conceit we

Workshop at National Theatre School. Photographer unknown.

were investigating involved my own presence on stage as myself, alongside an actor playing "me." Theatre and performance were intrinsic aspects of the text, given the correlation between a courtroom and a theatre, my transcribed cross-examination on the stand involving myriad theatrical analogies, and the very fact of our sharing this story on the stage.

Chris brought the developing script to the National Theatre School in Montreal. The graduating class of students took on the investigation with extraordinary commitment and energy. This workshop with these talented and inspiring students fully informed the script's next draft which led to the public presentation that Chris directed at The Theatre Centre.

Brett Donahue

Actor involved in the development of *Out the Window* between 2010 and 2018:

My experience with this play runs from its first footing as a play workshop while I was an acting student at NTS, its first professional production in 2012 at The Theatre Centre, and finally, to its reimagined version presented at the Luminato Festival of 2018. The beauty of my time with this piece has been seeing its evolution; both within my experience of it, and as it has refined and expanded upon itself to greater serve the discussion it provokes.

For me, the play started as an exercise in verbatim theatre. An investigation in dramaturgy; trying to sift through the boxes of transcripts looking for some sort of arc, writing accompanying viewpoints, and loosely blocking a sort of "presentation" which only a select few would see. Building on this experience, Liza formulated the 2012 play, which I performed in. It was miles away from our first experience in the basement of a theatre school, yet what lingered after our run was that the play still wasn't enough. Being "stuck" was the resounding feeling I had when walking away from that first production. We'd addressed something, but to no real resolution. We'd spoken out about a system and its repercussions, but nothing more would come of it.

When I was approached to be a part of the Luminato production, I was hesitant. The team assembled was a dream, but I couldn't help but wonder how we'd jump that hurdle of unfulfillment. What ultimately resolved my hesitation was the company's commitment to expansion. Not only with the size and technical capabilities of the space in which we would play and what that would allow, but more so with the people involved in telling the story. And this, for me, is how the piece transcended. In 2018, we were able to create what the play was meant to be. Not just the depiction of a man's life ending in tragedy at the hands of the police, but a conversation with the public about the insufficiency of policing mental health, and the flagrant shortcomings of our justice system and those individuals who are meant to uphold it. During my first two experiences with the show, although great efforts had been made to create a discussion around this story for an audience, it remained a theatrical exercise because the individuals tasked in telling it were actors in a theatre. With the involvement of artists, activists, experts and individuals actually living the issues discussed throughout our show, the piece itself could fully serve its purpose. The show's voice became one of authenticity that used the events confined within the transcripts as a sort of foundation; a gathering place where an exploration of issues surrounding mental health, policing and the justice system could unfold. What started as words isolated on the page became a real discussion: extensive, inclusive, profound, and broad.

The script for the 2010 workshop presentation, directed by Chris with assistant director Philip McKee, included an extensive amount of the verbatim material uncovered during these months of research and development. The officers' testimony between 2002 and 2006 filled the action of the play. Much of this same material continued to be included in the 2012 and 2018 productions.

From Act II:
LAWYER 2:
Now, sir, there's something called a code of silence or a "Blue Code of Silence" among officers. Police officers develop, for obvious reasons, a kind of camaraderie when they work together.

OFFICER A:
Of course. It's a job. Like any other, I guess.

LAWYER 2:
Sometimes there are tense situations when police officers work together and they are called upon to use force against other human beings, right?

OFFICER A:
If you have to, yes.

LAWYER 2:
And there's at least the potential that some officers might use excessive force in some situations, right?

OFFICER A:
In some situations, but not this situation.

LAWYER 2:
I'm talking more generally now.

OFFICER A:
I can't comment on hypotheticals. But to agree with your hypothetical, maybe, yeah.

LAWYER 2:
There are a couple of lawyer jokes that come to mind but I'm going to refrain. Sir, have you heard any case where

a police officer reported another police officer for using excessive force?

OFFICER A:
I can't say if I have or haven't.

LAWYER 2:
Well, you can say you have or haven't, sir. Have you—

OFFICER A:
I've heard—again, this is speculation and rumours. But I have heard over the years that other police officers might have. I heard of one situation where they didn't understand why the person had to use force. Years ago.

LAWYER 2:
Are you saying that an officer reported another officer for that, sir?

OFFICER A:
I don't say "reported," but he was concerned why force was used.

LAWYER 2:
Like, for example, if you had seen your partner hitting Mr. Vass on the legs as he described in court and you had thought that was excessive, you might have to say to him, quietly, hey, maybe next time you don't have to keep on hitting him that much. You could back off a little bit, right?

OFFICER A:
If that scenario took place, in a perfect world, I would have stopped him. But I didn't see him do any of that.

LAWYER 2:
Right. You didn't see him hitting at all?

OFFICER A:
So I can't comment on that.

LAWYER 2:
But I'm suggesting that you would never, ever, ever, report to any authorities that he had to use excessive force, in your view. That's what you would never do and that's what the code of silence precludes.

OFFICER A:
I disagree with you, sir,

LAWYER 2:
You disagree.

OFFICER A:
I joined this job—I have a lot of integrity. I joined this job to help people… am I saying that it never happens? No. No. But I've never in the ten years of my being a police officer, had occasions to have that come across. The "Blue Code of Silence" or what do you call it? The blue or code of silence, wouldn't affect me. It's not something that police officers talk about if there is a code of silence…they are just normal everyday people that have families like everyone else and you just do your job.

This version of the show involved the inclusion of some non-verbatim text, newly created scenes that I had written. They became a kind of play within a play. Among them was a terrifying scene inspired by some of my own concerns about the Toronto police force learning of this production. At this point, I don't believe I had had any interviews with the Deputy Chief of Police at the time, something that became part of the research for the project's next iteration.

Entitled "Nightmare Scenario," this totally imaginary scene took place in a bar where "Liza" was a waitress. Four officers arrived, ordered drinks and were reading over an ad for the show in Toronto's *NOW Magazine*. The scene grew violent, a reflection of the protagonist's—and my—private fears early on. The scene was powerfully realized by the talented cast of actors involved, with me watching alongside on stage.

A chunk of the feedback generated from this showing pointed toward the script's vibrancy, but also its challenges. Among them: ME. Me, onstage, both playing myself and publicly witnessing. This was not about my "acting" per se—I'm a good actor—but rather, my presence. It distracted from the greater story itself. If people were wondering about how I was doing, instead of watching the action of the play… if they were wondering if this were some form of public therapy for me, then… I had to go, as it were. This made great sense to me and also, truth be told, it came as a relief.

Another essential question emerged: What was the play about? The response was overwhelmingly positive: The project investigated multiple themes and was very compelling. BUT. What was the play's arc; its journey? This was a legitimate question. I am using the word "play" here a lot. A PLAY has, or generally strives to have, a clear narrative involving a beginning, middle and end. This version, with marvellous actors and some incendiary new—and older—material was strong. And Chris's vision was viscerally wild, complex, and rich. But where to go with it next?

A confession: I was stuck. I remained stuck. This was embarrassing to admit. But there it was. In fact, I was so embarrassed that I withdrew. I wasn't able to share this creative, murky stickiness with Chris. This proved problematic. Understandably so. Chris had a number of other projects in development. We had gone as far as we could go together.

A second confession: This is what happens when a creator of a compelling project isn't quite up to or perhaps really ready for, either artistically or emotionally, the subject matter and a collaboration with an artist of Chris's calibre and practice.

In retrospect, I admit to not having had enough knowledge and/or trust in myself as an artist or person to continue to be a productive collaborator. This was one piece of the puzzle. The other piece was something that would remain hidden for a little while longer: *Out the Window* wasn't created to be a "play" in the usual sense of the word. No. It IS a play—and a communal conversation—about a horrific subject that as yet, has no end…

I am forever grateful to Chris and Crow's for opening up this project in ways I could have never imagined when I began.

Works-in-Progress Class, University of Windsor, 2011

The focus of this five-week session was an investigation of verbatim theatre, with an eventual focus on material from *Out the Window*. This was an opportunity to introduce the genre to the students. We began the session by researching productions of plays created using verbatim text. *Out the Window* was eventually introduced, and the students were then encouraged not only to dive into working with the specific text, and researching its multiple themes, but also create their own short works in response to the material. Their thrilling, provocative creations were filled with movement, soundscape, scenography and text.

This course exemplified what I have always hoped for this project: That the material sparks further artistic inquiry into the multiple themes embedded in its storytelling. This publication strives to open up this possibility.

University of Windsor. Photo by Liza Balkan.

The Theatre Centre 2012

Out the Window lay dormant for a couple of years until Franco Boni invited it to be included in The Theatre Centre's Free Fall Festival in 2012. Aislinn Rose, who had been involved in the script's development with Crow's, rejoined the project and the team of collaborators.

For this iteration, I returned to using primarily verbatim rather than created text. I also removed myself from the body of the show. I introduced the piece and then left the stage until its final moment. This moment is realized on film in the 2018 production. I vowed never to be onstage again in this piece.

(You will note in the full script included in this book that I withdrew this vow. Director Sarah Garton Stanley and Assistant Director Tanisha Taitt were highly persuasive. I caved in. But not without a fight!)

By 2012, the amount of research material accumulated for the *Out the Window* was extensive: hundreds of pages of court transcripts, transcribed interviews with lawyers, cops, activists, psychiatrists, police psychologists and family members of the deceased. Alongside the above was the national—and North America-wide—reportage of incidents and investigations into police violence. Among my goals for the project was to generate and share as much information and perspective as possible. I believed that this might provoke more robust conversations about this multi-layered topic. At this point, the project was five years old. The deeper I went down this tentacled rabbit hole of research and discovery, the more Bankers Boxes were added to those lining my walls. My brain was exploding. Included in the din was the impossible question: How to include it all in a single, two-and-a-half-hour production that would hopefully keep the audience leaning forward. Producer and collaborator Aislinn Rose came up with an inspiring solution, one that would allow this material to find its way into the production itself and become a public resource for the audience outside The Theatre Centre's walls.

Aislinn Rose

Artistic Director, The Theatre Centre

(The following is an excerpt originally written for theatre blog praxistheatre.com in anticipation of the opening week of *Out the Window* at The Theatre Centre in 2012.)

Out the Window opens one week from today.

I started working on Liza Balkan's *Out the Window* in 2010 when I was invited by Chris Abraham to join a development and workshop phase with Crow's Theatre. I was in the very early stages of examining my own project that involved court transcripts, interviews and verbatim text, so it was an ideal project for me to observe.

I had no idea at the time that I would go on to work with Liza over the next couple of years, providing dramaturgical support at first, and then creating my most complicated online project next: The Brain.

Out the Window chronicles the years Liza spent making her way through the Canadian justice system after witnessing the death of Otto Vass after an altercation with the police in 2000. The piece also examines the years after the 2006 inquest, during which Liza has conducted countless interviews with lawyers, activists, police, and members of the community.

Throughout those years, Liza has accumulated several Bankers Boxes, hundreds of computer files, and DVDs, CDs, and mini DV cassettes filled with research, testimonies, and the work created by designers, actors and other artists. As I worked with Liza, it became apparent to me that this vast amount of content needed to be archived somehow, and preferably in a way that would make it accessible to the public. Enter: The Brain.

As Artistic Producer of Praxis Theatre, I have long been interested in experimenting with methods of interacting with potential audience members in the lead-up to a show, and in continuing the conversations sparked by the show's content after the show has ended. For *Out the Window* I proposed the creation of an "online brain" that would allow me to try to capture Liza's knowledge, along with the history of the project, in an interactive tool that would provide the public with an opportunity to navigate the immense amount of information according to their own interests.

Using mind-mapping software, I have created four main sub-sections that branch off into a myriad of different sibling and child "thoughts." Some thoughts contain embedded photos and PDFs, while others contain links to articles and documents. The Brain is a work-in-progress with a huge amount of information still to come.

I have also created an online home for the project where you can read about the show, the artists involved, and take a look at an introductory post about The Brain that provides some how-to advice on navigation.

One of the other things we've been exploring with our work at Praxis Theatre is how our online activities can directly impact the development of our work. I am very excited to see how the creation of The Brain has had an impact on *Out the Window*. In addition to The Brain having found its way into the design of the show itself, with the existence of our living archive, we've been able to make peace with the elimination of certain sections of text or design work, knowing that these elements would go on to have a life online.

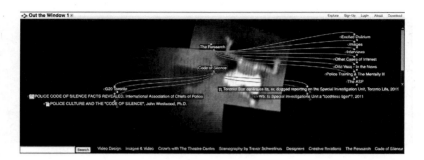

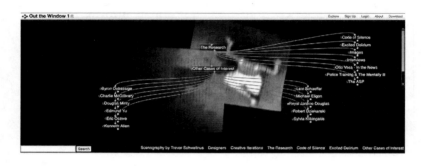

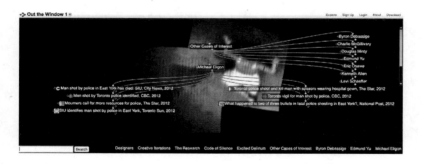

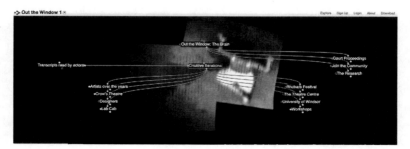

The Brain was an intrinsic part of the process and provided an immersive, communal sharing of vast amounts of material and research that demanded to be seen. Aislinn continued to upload material after the show closed. Unfortunately, the funding necessary to carry on increasing The Brain's capacity ran out. Sadly, this incredible digital warehouse no longer exists. In 2012/2013, the material returned to the analog of the Bankers Box.

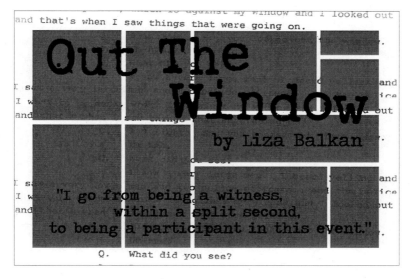

The quotation on this postcard belongs to one of the officers. It always felt, however, like an all-encompassing phrase for this project: Witness to participant; the actions of the officers, the protagonist of the play, and also the audience itself. They became active participants in this production.

The year leading up to this production involved extending my interviews to lawyers, activists, a leading police psychologist, members of the police force, a deputy chief of police in Toronto… Transcripts from these interviews were woven into a second of three acts. The goal in adding this wealth of material was to provide the audience with enough information—beyond their possible biases and beliefs—leading to the possibility of a more informed and thus more productive conversation.

The night before opening, however, it became clear that this endeavour would lead to overload for an audience. It was too long. Too much information. Important information, yes, but the goal was to keep an audience leaning forward. The multiple perspectives added to this second act ultimately weighed down the storytelling. The third act demanded much attention from the audience. So, that night before opening, the company sat together, and we cut much of what was ostensibly a year's worth of interviews and creation of new material and dramaturgy. Heartbreaking. Necessary. I am forever grateful to Franco and Aislinn and the entire, über-generous company of artists, for their willingness to shift so radically the night before an opening!

Excerpt from 2012 script:

ACT I
The following text is 98% court transcripts and interviews. The rest is grappling with the intangibles of memory and truth.

> *We are in a theatre. We see the bare walls, the lights, the sound technician, etc. This is a theatre in its own state, without the trappings of any obvious "set." There is one large table constructed of two good-sized tables placed together, eight chairs surrounding it. There are microphones and music stands, a bike... all placed randomly around the space. The walls are lined with Bankers Boxes. The creator of the project, Liza Balkan*, is there chatting informally with the audience. Seven other individuals enter sporadically and head to their various seats at the table. These actors acknowledge each other, can acknowledge any audience members they may know. The feeling is informal and the houselights are still up. The actors playing/reading the OFFICERS are dressed casually in comfortable street clothes. The actor playing LAWYER 1 is a bit more formally dressed, the actor playing LAWYER 2, less so.*

> *There are three very large multi-paned windows above the playing space. The "panes" are various sizes and are asymmetrical. Images and words/information will be*

projected onto these screens at various times during the performance.

The text — court testimony — in Acts I and III is read. Act II, the actors are "off book."

*It is important to note that the real Liza Balkan will not be "acting," but rather "hosting," providing a few details which "fill in the gaps" before the action begins. An actor will play "Liza" during the rest of show. The "Real" Liza will not be seen during the action of the piece, until the final moment of Act III.

The actor playing Liza wears a body microphone, which is used during specific moments of the action and cross-examination.

Once all are assembled — the audience and performers alike — and Liza Balkan has briefly checked in with them all, the show begins.

"Real" Liza looks around at the audience, acknowledging their presence. She carries a large round roll of yellow police caution tape.

She lays the tape down on the floor as she addresses the audience, separating the audience from the playing area.

REAL LIZA:
Hi. Welcome. My Name is Liza. Thank you for coming.

She reminds the volunteers to meet with her during the intermission. They have been chosen earlier, unless one more is still needed to fill the quota of six. In which case, she will ask for another volunteer then and there. Once that is done, she continues:

REAL LIZA:
Two important details:

1. Everything you're about to hear has been culled from court testimony and interviews. Verbatim: the truth and nothing but the truth.

Except for what isn't.

2. There will be snacks.

The caution taping is finished.

On August 9th, 2000, the daily joke at www.dailyjoke.com was: (*She reads.*) "The advantage of a bad memory is that one enjoys several times the same good things for the first time." Friedrich Nietzsche.

>*Cymbal clash: Ba da BOOM.*

>*Beat.*

Let's begin.

>*Sudden shift in lights: Darkness, flashing red police lights, crime scene ambiance, multiple shadows, which constantly shift perspective and focus.*

>*SOUND: Police siren, ambulance, crime scene ambiance.*

The vision for this production included the act of the audience witnessing the reading of transcripts. The above photos are from Act I wherein we see the officers as young men—out of uniform.

In Act II, we invited six members of the audience to join us onstage for a meal. The actors playing officers became waiters. The text of the meal was created from excerpts from an extended lunch I had had with two of the lawyers involved—one from each "side." I was given permission to tape that conversation. "Witness to participant" guided this choice. This was totally interesting and provocative, but not entirely successful. At least, not until the final performance wherein the actors involved—Julie Tepperman, RH Thomson, and David Ferry began to ask those at the table about their perspectives on the events. Conversations were a bit awkward and personal—and fascinating. Had we had more time (we had only approximately ten days of rehearsal) we might have investigated this idea more fully. Regardless, I sensed this was a concept worth including. A payoff came at the end of the luncheon: the servers returned in their police uniforms—for the first time in the show. The audience would experience their own personal shifts around witnessing the physical transformation of these four young men. How does a police uniform alter our response to the human wearing it? What happens to the human who dons the outfit? This was an attempt at a kind of subliminal investigation of one aspect of police culture at work.

The workshop production at The Theatre Centre played to full houses and included post-show discussions involving activists, lawyers, psychologists, and members of the police force. One particularly electrifying moment occurred when Otto Vass's wife, Zsuzsanna, stood up and spoke to the crowd and panelists, which included then Deputy Chief of Police, Mike Federico, and activist and former mayor of Toronto, John Sewell. She shared halting words about her husband, about his death and her experiences with the justice system. Afterwards, Sewell introduced her to Federico—a first meeting for them both. Names and numbers become human.

That night I also learned a very hard lesson about verbatim text and the responsibility, care, and due diligence it demands. I had gone to what I felt had been extraordinary lengths to establish and uphold all of the above. I failed miserably in one key area.

Zsuzsanna brought her son, now 18 years old, to the show. He had been only around eight years old when his father died that summer night. I had interviewed them both for this project. In fact, I had met with Zsuzsanna several times over the course of a few years.

Included in this showing was a section of court transcript involving the final arguments from one of the defence lawyers for the police. His powerful words described Voss as mentally unstable and volatile, listing past violent incidents on public record to support his argument. I included this section as a way in which to highlight the legal system's propensity for using a victim's historical behaviour as proof of their own culpability, the victim as criminal.

After the show, Zsuzsanna told me that her son had never before heard about these prior violent incidents involving his father. He was shaken. Understandably. I realized immediately that I had—my choice had—messed him up. I had not thought to warn about nor discuss the inclusion of this text with them. Shit. I apologized profusely for this error on my part and promised to edit this particular section. I did so for the following performances. This didn't change the fact that my project had forever altered this young man's relationship with the memory of his father. This young man who had so generously allowed me to interview him about his dad.

I removed verbatim text highlighting a horrifically unjust, regular practice in the justice system, out of respect for the humans involved. Was this the right thing to do? Most importantly, I should have done the right thing earlier. Hard lesson learned about the ethics of verbatim play creation—at the cost of a young man and his mother. Shit. I continued to be in touch with Zsuszanna in the years following. She attended the show in 2018. Her son did not.

The workshop production in 2012 at The Theatre Centre, which I directed along with associate director Shari Hollett, included audience participation in the form of six members from each audience joining the actors onstage for a meal during Act II, which was an edited transcription of a lunch in a restaurant in Toronto that I had attended with two lawyers involved in the case.

2012 Production. Zahir Gilani, Jason Siks, Julie Tepperman, Brett Donahue. Photo by Abhishek Chandra.

Inquest. Photo by Abhishek Chandra.

2012. The Lunch.

Luminato Festival 2018

The production of the project at the Luminato Festival in Toronto in 2018, under the guidance of director Sarah Garton Stanley, incorporated a goodly portion of the material shared in 2012 and then brilliantly expanded the storytelling to include extensive community engagement, an art gallery, a choir, food, and conversation.

Syrus Marcus Ware

Vanier Scholar, visual artist, activist, curator, and educator. Luminato production live artist.

I started organizing in the '90s, doing Mad justice work and psych survivor organizing. I remember Otto Vass's case and his death and the trial. I remember the Justice for Otto Vass Committee. I remember this case that rocked our worlds in the early 2000s and I am thankful that his name was remembered and reinserted into public dialogue nearly twenty years later through this production. I remember so much from *Out the Window*, a verbatim theatre production by Liza Balkan and directed by Sarah Garton Stanley, with assistant director Tanisha Taitt, for Luminato 2018.

We met in New York City in fall of 2017 and experimented—the musical duo LAL (Nic Murray and Rosina Kazi) and Sarah Kitz who had been cast as Liza Balkan. We met daily in this warehouse space down by the old World Trade Center site— in a spacey environment where we played with projections, Go-Pro cameras, drawing on the floor, and a storm of emotion for the climax of the play.

Months later we began rehearsals fully, working with the cast as spring blossomed in Tkaronto. My part of the performance was very physical— it involved me drawing on my knees for about an hour before moving into interactive performance art with the audience in the final act. For our rehearsals, I drew countless portraits while we practised, always of the same image—Otto Vass, in his white tuxedo and ruffled shirt, beaming at the camera at some kind of fancy function. I drew Vass every day for months, reflecting on policing, Madness, and the justice system while I drew.

I am a prison and police abolitionist, and have been for 25 years. In this production, I got to explore policing and its implications on Mad people. I got to work with a team curious about Mad justice and wanting an end to the Blue Code of Silence and the targeted policing that led to cases like Vass's.

By the time it got to opening week, spring had turned to early summer and we were doing dress and tech rehearsals. I still remember the first time we practised the culminating action of Act II, wherein the police officers in formal dress uniforms pick up my drawing of Vass from the floor, like a coffin, and carry it to the rear of the stage where they then mount it in amongst a wall of drawings I'd created of Mad people killed by the police: Edmund Yu, Amleset Hailie, Andrew Loku and others. It was striking and bold and powerful directing—exactly what I would expect from the incredible Sarah Garton Stanley and Tanisha Taitt.

Together, the whole team co-created a third act that involved interaction with the audience where we got to address alternatives to policing in cases of crisis, conflict and harm and possibilities for Mad people—if we let Mad people be Mad in public space, and if we didn't call the cops on them simply for being Mad in public.

I will never forget the nightly discussions with local activists about abolition and Madness and activism. I will never forget the process for this development, building a project together over a year and making something profoundly timely, political and personal.

This performance took place at Luminato right in the end of the "before times" (pre-pandemic). Before the pandemic, before the uprisings of 2020, before the recent turn towards anti-policing and abolition. I would love to experience this production now—or in the near future—with audiences now tuned in and turned on to abolition and the idea that police aren't always the protectors that TV and movies portray them to be.

I am profoundly thankful to the entire creative team, cast and crew, and of course to Liza, for creating this brilliant work.

Afterword
Naomi Campbell

Once Liza Balkan looked out the window of her apartment on Lansdowne Avenue on August 9, 2000, the show *Out the Window* was pretty much inevitable.

To witness is to be ever changed by an unbidden experience—to be caught by bad timing, good timing, luck or chance. Liza certainly did not plan to change her life that hot summer's night, but that's what happened. I was there too—asleep in the apartment two doors down the hall from Liza, also with a perfect view of the 7-Eleven parking lot. I have often wished I'd been awake, that I'd seen it all. Not because I want to have witnessed the beating death of Otto Vass, but because I could have corroborated Liza's story, because I believe her.

Very soon after it happened it was obvious to me that Liza would turn her experience into theatre. What else could she do? So many stories emerged, from the night itself to the days in court, from all her dealings with the police, and with lawyers, she had so much to share. The theatre provided a space for Liza to process her experience and transform it into something that could be witnessed by the audience, and so, perhaps, could ease her burden by creating more witnesses.

I think that Nightswimming, the dramaturgical theatre company where I was producer at the time—gave Liza the first bit of money so that she could start purchasing the many boxes of court transcripts she needed to figure out the story. So many words; so much paper!

Some shows take a long time to find themselves, but from that first installation performance at Factory Theatre in 2007 it was clear to me that Liza was on to something really important, and while it took years to complete the task, the Theatre Centre co-production of *Out the Window* with Luminato in 2018 was well worth the wait. By then the depth of understanding that Liza and her collaborators had acquired, the detail and authority of her research, the authenticity of the voices, all made for a rich, complex experience for the audience to witness. The full power of the community that Liza accumulated over the years she worked on the project was fully evident in the final production, which was big and bold and radical, and yet held at its heart the essence of Liza's experience that night in August 2000. Like memory, it had shifted and changed along the way through retelling and interpretation, but that is the theatre, after all.

I am grateful that I could support Liza in some small ways over the years and am so pleased that *Out the Window* is being published so that the conversations it inspires can continue.

Naomi Campbell is the Artistic Director Luminato Festival, Toronto's International Festival of Arts and Ideas.

Mind. The. Gap.

a gap
a space
an aperture
a crack
a crevice.
A hole
in recollection
You see that?
An opening
A breach
A blank
to be filled in
You see that?
Oh—
Did you see that?!
The gap is the sensate.
It is the careening adrenalin
Of time crashing still
While whipping forward
The gap
contains the shock of the blow.
It holds the *flesh* of the flash of a moment
And its echoes.
Okay
Litigation demands the articulation of how
Something
Some *one*
Goes from being breath to being data.
How do you codify the coda of a heartbeat?
Okay.
In the crack of recollection
is the juncture
of the puncture of a son
and of a home.
The gap is brimming with savage scenery
Every vista
Each perspective

(It is) The view when lying on the pavement
Looking up while being pummelled,
(It is) The view when looking down as your foot kicks his face
(It is) The landscape from the railing on the porch across the
way
(It is) the *air,* five flights above
between my hands on the glass and the parking lot below.
It is both crystalline and incoherent all at once.
The gap
contains the shock of the blow.
It holds the *flesh* of the flash of a moment
And its echoes.
What lives in this chasm between language and legitimacy?
I can tightrope across the divide.
But *fill* it?
It's already *full* to capacity.
There's no room at the inn.
What with
memory and longing and smell and touch and sight
and blood and puke and Netflix
and loss and hope and fright
All standing in line jostling for space.
There's no room.
How do you analyze and legitimize
The *mist* between a scream and sirens?
The *gasp* of information dropping?
The *choice* in its act of forming?
The landscape of the gap is jagged terrain
it is pre-historic.
We're talking tectonic plates here.
But I was taught in wiki-school
that boundaries between plates are often ill-defined.
They are hidden beneath the oceans.
Exactly.
Hidden beneath *emotions*
Eroding upon contact.
Dissolving in the very moment of translation.
The gap is the *sensate.*
It's the careening adrenalin
Of time crashing still

As it whips forward
it is pre-inhalation.
You see that?
What fills the gap is the *truth* of the *sensation*.
Attempting to articulate the inarticulate
Will only obfuscate
And obliterate
its contents.
The gap is *overflowing* with the consequence
Of the impotence
of language.

— Liza Balkan

Thank You!

A few members of the village involved in the development of
Out the Window at various times between 2007 and 2018:

Chris Abraham
Stewart Arnott
Marc Aubin
Sean Baker
Tom Barnett
Franco Boni
Christine Brubaker
Buddies in Bad Times/Rhubarb Festival
Claire Calnan
Charles Campbell
Naomi Campbell
Jennifer Chambers
Derrick Chua
Gary Clewley
Paul Copeland
Mason Coulter
Crows Theatre
Steve Cumyn
Ishan Dave
Bob Dodds
Brett Donahue
Frank Donato
Matt Donovan
Roxanne Duncan
Peter Eaton
Factory Theatre/Lab Cab
Mike Federico
Andrew Ferguson
David Ferry
David Fox
Murray Furrow
Stephen Gartner
Lwam Ghebrehariat
Zahir Gilani
Dr. David Goldbloom

James Graham
Richard Greenblatt
Gillian Hards
Michael Healey
Shari Hollett
Rosina Kazi
Robert Kennedy
Nadeem Umar Khitab
Sarah Kitz
Richard Lee
Luminato Festival
Montgomery Martin
Philip McKee
Allyson McMackon
Jeff Meadows
Jim Mezon
Matt Murray
Nicholas Murray
National Theatre School, 2010 Class
Mellisa Novokosky
Philip Nozaku
Thomas Ryder Payne
Sandy Plunkett
Emily Porter
Geoffrey Pounsett
Kyle Purcell
Michelle Ramsay
Josephine Ridge
Peyson Rock
Aislinn Rose
Peter Rosenthal
Warren Scheffer
Trevor Schwellnus
John Sewell
Jason Siks
Stephen Sparks
Bojana Stancic
Sarah Garton Stanley
Sean Sullivan
Lilya Sultanova

Anita Szigeti
Tanisha Taitt
Jennifer Tarver
Julie Tepperman
The Theatre Centre
RH Thomson
University of Windsor, 2012 2nd Year Acting Class
Rebecca Vandevelde
Michael Vass
Zsuszanna Vass
Syrus Marcus Ware
Anna Willats
Billy Wolf
Ming Wong

Thank you to those who prefer to remain anonymous.

And finally, my sincere apologies to anyone who was involved in the project over its many years whose name I may have forgotten to list above. Call me. Let me know, so I can offer a huge, grateful thank you!